THOM HARINCK

GODFATHER OF MUAY THAI KICKBOXING IN
THE WEST

JULIO PUNCH
THOM HARINCK

/\P

In loving memory of Richard Ploos and Iwan de Randamie

*Chakuriki students and their sensei mourn the tragic death of
Iwan de Randamie*

CONTENTS

PREFACE

In the late 1970s several shows taking place in the Far East were broadcast on Dutch Television, like *Sandokan* and *Kris Pusaka*. As a little boy these shows captured my imagination about the mystical East and of course eastern martial arts. During a six-month stay in Albany (New York) in 1981, I discovered a kung fu club on Central Avenue. It later turned out to be owned by an American lady with red hair and a Chinese name. It was not long before I joined and my first lesson soon followed. It was the start of my training in martial arts that continued through most of the 1980s and resulted in achieving a blue belt in kyokushinkai karate under sensei Kenneth Leeuwin (World Karate Champion with the WUKO in 1986).

When I returned to the Netherlands, there seemed to be a different martial arts climate to what I had experienced in the US. Kickboxing seemed to be getting a lot of attention with three gyms being at the forefront: Vos Gym, Mejiro Gym and Chakuriki Gym. All three of them were situated in Amsterdam. Of the three gyms Chakuriki was the most noticeable in Amsterdam's street life. You could often see people walking around with Chakuriki T-shirts or track suits. When I went to my first kickboxing event in Amsterdam's *Jaap Edenhal* at the age of 17, there were - besides those from Amsterdam - fighters from Breda and Rotterdam (see list of sports halls in Appendix C). The sport was spreading all over the country. While some coaches came and went, there was one name that was a mainstay as far as kickboxing was concerned. That name was Thom Harinck.

In 2012 I was toying with the idea of writing a book. I had already written articles for my websites for a number of years. Several of the Dutch kickboxing champions, Ernesto Hoost and Remy Bonjasky among them, already had biographies written about their lives. Thom Harinck, the man who had witnessed the development of kickboxing from the sport's infancy, still had no biography. I sent Thom Harinck an email and he soon replied. We met in the gym a week later where he was training the competition group and decided that English would be the chosen language, so we could reach more people. Thom dropped by my house and started telling me his story which I recorded. It was the first of many meetings in which Thom would recount stories from the 40+ years he was active as a coach. I would translate it into English and that is how this book came to be. The story is essentially Thom recounting his experiences, with occasional comments from me. The tone of these memoirs is therefore conversational. I have added appendices describing the various forms of martial arts and added a list of stadiums and of Japanese terms.

To protect the privacy of certain individuals, some names in the text have been changed. Some events recounted have been covered in detail in the Dutch media and are hence in the public domain.

It is my hope that this book inspires you to realise your dreams, whatever they may be.

I would like to thank my parents, Corry and Maurice Punch and

Roger Price for proofreading, and Maurice and Roger again for kindly writing an introduction.

Julio Punch, Amstelveen.

INTRODUCTION

The Netherlands has in recent decades adopted martial arts with enthusiasm and success: and one man, Thom Harinck, is largely responsible for their adoption and growth. Harinck has a remarkable record of grooming champions. This makes him the Dutch equivalent for martial arts of the renowned coaches Sir Alex Ferguson (football) or Vince Lombardi (American football): and Harinck also deserves high praise for his achievements. These were not only in shaping top performers but also in coaching many ordinary boys and young men whose lives were improved by his mentorship. Why he has not received the awards seen in other sports is related to several factors which will be addressed below, before turning to his life's work and successes. But first we shall touch briefly on the development of sports in society to put the story of Harinck and martial arts in the Netherlands in a broader context.

There is wide evidence of games being played in many early societies. These could hardly be described as "sports" as they could be extremely violent and even fatal for competitors. In the Mexican Maya complexes, for example, there were sports fields for teams to play a ball game, but the losing team then faced execution! And in the Roman arena, slaves and prisoners would fight deadly battles as gladiators for the amusement of the imperial elite and the public. In medieval cities and villages, moreover, there were diverse games, sometimes involving possession of a ball or object, which could last several days with intense rivalry and large numbers of participants. The Iroquois Indians in Canada and the US were found by settlers to be playing a game, that later developed as lacrosse, with up to 1,000 participants and lasting two to three days. Some early sports, like football games in the streets of old London, led to cracked heads and broken bones. So sports and games could be rough, tough and dangerous and have few rules.

In contrast, the Greeks had introduced athletic sports, and the first Olympic Games, as a celebration of the human body allied to competition but without violence. That attitude later helped to civilize games in nineteenth-century Europe when various sports associations began to develop rules for the size of teams, length of play, points to be won, conduct during the game and control through a referee or umpire. Initially these newly regulated games were typically for the amateur teams of the elite with a strong spirit of "sportsmanship" and mostly for men. From those origins there then emerged professional sports for large audiences in stadiums with large crowds and salaried players. Many of these sports have developed global associations with universally accepted rules with the main example being football / "soccer". This is played all over the world and is regulated by one agency, FIFA (*Fédération Internationale de Football Association*).

Other sports - including athletics, cricket, rugby, lacrosse, tennis, golf, badminton, hockey, fencing, squash and sailing, and especially in the US, baseball, basketball and "grid-iron" football - were also exported to those continents influenced by western societies in their expansion: Africa, Asia, South America and Australia/New Zealand.

In Asia, however, there was already a complex range of very different sports almost unknown in the West apart from judo and jiu-jitsu. These sports emerged from the exercises of warriors like the Japanese *samurai*, but had a vastly different culture and organizational structure to the western sports. But after the Second World War, they too began to attract massive public attention and major commercial interests, particularly in Japan and Thailand. It was only around the 1970s that these "martial arts" began to make significant inroads in Europe and North America with the Netherlands playing a key role. Let's look, then, at the role of martial arts in that country and also explain why Harinck has been so successful, yet has not been granted the status of successful coaches in other sports.

First, martial arts are not a major sport in the Netherlands in certain respects (reflected in the number of registered members) and certainly not compared to their standing in several Asian countries, although they have brought the nation much success. The top five of registered members of sports associations are football, tennis, golf, hockey and fishing. The Dutch are clearly a sporting nation with about half the population of 18 million taking some form of exercise: and they are tall! They tend to be more successful at team sports – football (soccer), (field)hockey, rowing, cycling and volleyball – than at the more "individual" sports. They have produced top performers in swimming, speed skating, show-jumping and sailing but less so in athletics (although that is changing) and tennis. That team element could be related to the fact that the Dutch are group-oriented "joiners" with a wealth of clubs and associations. So there are many people involved in sport across a broad range of disciplines and those sports activities are highly regulated.

It's also evident that a handful of sports dominate the media. There is always vast coverage of the Dutch football team, Dutch riders in the *Tour De France* and skaters (in speed skating but also in the famous "Eleven City Race"/*Elfstedentocht*, which is a gruelling race of 200 kilometres on ice, linking eleven cities in Friesland). The folk heroes are typically from those three sports with Johan Cruijff (renowned football player) as the leading, and most voluble, icon. Occasionally one emerges in other sports: Fanny Blankers-Koen (the "Flying Housewife") was immortalised when she won four gold medals in athletics at the 1948 Olympic Games in London. And, importantly, Anton Geesink won the world championship in judo in 1961 and the gold medal in the Olympics of 1964 in Japan. Geesink was the first westerner who showed that the Japanese could be defeated on their own territory at a sport they had dominated and at which they were long considered invincible. That they could compete in the Asian-dominated sports was a highly significant message to those who took up judo and other martial arts in the West. But it is clear that far less attention is being paid to martial arts and it attracts less funding and commercial interest than other sports in the Netherlands.

Secondly, the martial arts throughout the world display a bewildering variety of forms and styles across regions and within countries and it has proven difficult to regulate the sports centrally. For outsiders it is difficult to decipher what the diverse forms mean in terms of specific styles and how widely they are practised and performed. There is none of the uniformity and clarity that surround the major sports in the West. Hence the institutional framework is confusingly varied and fragmented with no equivalent of FIFA for the martial arts.

Thirdly, the basic unit is the individual *dojo* led by a central figure - referred to as *sensei* (teacher) - who is revered for his wisdom and experience. This makes relationships both local and highly personal, with the primary basis being founded on personal affiliations and local attachments that cannot easily be transferred.

Fourthly, there has been a move away from physical "contact" sports in some societies. Some town councils in the UK, for instance, have banned boxing, rugby, football and martial arts from school sports in favour of golf, archery and racquet games (partly because they are usually cheaper). The contact sports are based on channelling the violence element into acceptable and supervised levels. However, as many such sports are played by young males in a competitive spirit, it can be that games lead to conflict and even injury. Sport can provide an arena for individual and group aggression. There is, for instance, considerable violence in amateur football in the Netherlands between players, between players and supporters and between players and referees, with one referee even being kicked to death recently. In several sports considerable efforts have been made to clean up the game. Rugby, for example, had a potential for illicit force in tackles and scrums but has moved to direct intervention by referees. Actions taken include immediate sanctions (yellow card for temporary banishment to the "sin-bin" and red-card for sending off) and the review of bad conduct through video evidence during the game or later. In brief, the contact sports do provide an opportunity for illicit use of force but most major sports have taken measures to keep the controlled aggression of competition within acceptable boundaries.

Fifthly, there is the fact that certain contact sports have long drawn people to legal and illegal fights – sometimes of an extreme nature. There is something appealing for people from all walks of life about the primitive confrontation of two men, or indeed two women, slugging it out in the ring or cage. The fighters are often from working class and / or ethnic backgrounds. For them it is an opportunity to earn a great deal of money and become folk heroes. In boxing the matches are often held in prestigious locations – Madison Square Garden in New York or the Royal Albert Hall in London – have glamorous celebrities at the ring side, attract a large TV audience and the boxers can earn millions. In Asian societies there is the same status, large audiences, media attention, hero worship and financial rewards for the martial arts as for boxing in Western societies. That is not the case for martial arts in the West, for some of the reasons given above – for instance that they are minority sports that have to compete with long-established majority sports – but also because of their reputation.

Sixthly, martial arts have in the eyes of some become associated with organized crime. In a number of sports the stakes are high – with large sums of money and prestige involved – and that can lead devious people to engage in bribery, match-fixing, manipulation of transfers and doping. And there have been major scandals in football, cycling and horse racing in recent years. Indeed FIFA and the IAAF (International Association of Athletics Federations) are currently both facing investigations following serious accusations. But boxing, wrestling and martial arts do especially tend to attract, alongside many ordinary people, some members of the "underworld" to their performances. It is well known that they seek bouncers and bodyguards from the ranks of pugilists.

In the Netherlands some of the people mentioned in this book have worked for people associated with the "underworld". This is not to say that they were involved in any illegitimate activities as they may just have been impressive doormen employed to keep order outside an establishment. At one stage, as mentioned in this book, a training gym was set up in the renowned *Casa Rosso* in the red-light district of Amsterdam when few other facilities were available. This was a popular sex and gambling club led by "Black Jopie" de Vries who was considered to be a leading figure in the capital's underworld. But in the tolerant Netherlands, his club thrived while he generously supported several sports. In recent years, however, there has been a campaign in city and even government circles to investigate the financial backing of martial arts events and even to ban events in some towns. This has been fuelled by media attention to cases of martial arts practitioners, also mentioned here, who have used their skills outside the ring leading to prosecution and media coverage. In brief, the martial arts have been surrounded by controversy in recent years and its reputation has suffered from this.

Taking all this into account, it is valuable to have this biographical sketch of a major pioneer of the martial arts who not only groomed champions, but who also worked according to the classic ideals of the Asian martial arts. Those arts were built on a philosophy with two foundation stones: one was personal control over the practice of violence and the other was to avoid using that violence outside the *dojo*. Along with that came an Asian culture and structure based on dedication to the task, the acceptance of discipline, respect for hierarchy and attachment to the mentor and to his club. This means involvement in such sports is highly inclusive and impacts on one's lifestyle with a sense of honour and commitment to the group's rules. Of importance here is that in its pure form, the martial arts are strongly geared towards control of violence, avoidance of violence outside of the sport and respect for the opponent. Also important is adherence to the rules, respect for umpires at tournaments, respect for and commitment to one's mentor, abhorrence of cheating, avoidance of drugs and stimulants and rejection of any outside interference. In essence, these are sports which are dead against undue violence, drugs, involvement in illegitimate activities and links with the underworld. It would be naïve to think that this has always been achieved in Asian societies and elsewhere but that commitment to an all-embracing philosophy is of the essence in positioning the martial arts against the negativism it sometimes attracts.

Indeed, it is precisely that philosophy, set of values and practices that shine through Thom Harinck's story. And he is ideally placed to recount the growth and development of the martial arts in the Netherlands. As a young boy he was once overpowered by a larger boy and set out to learn to defend himself. What is evident is that he learns fast, takes in what is going on around him and is resilient in pursuing his aims. Early on, matters were fairly primitive with few facilities and low rewards, but in 1972 he set up his own gym in Amsterdam. He developed his own style: *chakuriki*. This is a mixture of styles and draws on the strength and length of Dutch fighters whilst sporting outfits of his own design. It is clear from the interviews conducted in this publication that Harinck has an eye for talent, can motivate fighters, is shrewd in weighing up opponents and changing tactics, can prepare fighters for the big occasion and has a close relationship with his sportsmen and sportswomen. He is a friend, counsellor, trainer, mental coach and mentor. At times he allowed young men to sleep in the gym and do odd jobs in return for training. He demanded adherence to discipline, respect from his fighters and conformity to the rules of no conflicts in the gym. He called for no use of violence outside the *dojo*, no drugs and no cheating, and above all, no going behind his back. He was a hard man when crossed and not easily intimidated. So when some Ajax (an Amsterdam football club) fans published some vile abuse and threats against his wife, he tracked them down and "persuaded" them to retract the statements.

Early on, he had quick success in the Netherlands and elsewhere in Europe but failed miserably on his first venture in Thailand when all five Dutch fighters were beaten by their Thai opponents. Quickly learning from that, he changed tactics and prepared his competitors to the extent that they began to win some of the highest prizes in martial arts in the stadiums of Thailand and Japan. He became a household name, along with his style and sportsmen, in those countries and earned much respect. Some of his champions – including Peter Aerts, Branko Cikatić, Hesdy Gerges and Badr Hari – also gained recognition domestically (in one case, however, not for sporting reasons).

Harinck also helped to set up the World Muay Thai Association in 1984 and served as its president, and he is a founder of the Dutch Kickboxing Association (NKBB), the Dutch Muay Thai Association (MTBN) and the European Muay Thai Association (EMTA). He "retired" in 2013. Like all great coaches he held a mixture of determination, resilience, flexibility, entrepreneurship and showmanship, an eye for detail and a personal concern for the welfare of his students. The *sensei* in turn demanded dedication and respect, and when that was not forthcoming there could be friction. But he put martial arts - and Dutch martial arts - on to the world stage and he and his fighters are well known and respected abroad. Above all, he consistently displayed integrity in promoting the philosophy and ideals of oriental martial arts around fairness, respect and discipline and, most importantly, not using martial arts skills outside of the sporting arena.

Harinck may not have attracted the level of recognition granted to other sporting coaches in the Netherlands, but he has achieved much as clearly emerges from this publication. And he recounts his life, career, success and failures in a down-to-earth manner and with an eye for detail which typifies his personality. The interviews were recorded in Dutch and translated into English. Harinck sometimes uses typically "rich" Dutch idioms and slang, which are not always easy to convey in English. Harinck's legacy is to be seen in the thousands of young, and not so young, sportsmen and women who practice chakuriki-style kickboxing and other martial arts in accordance with the ideals of restrained violence and perfection of technique in sports clubs throughout the Netherlands. That's a significant accomplishment and it is well conveyed in this highly readable publication.

Roger Price and Maurice Punch, Maarssen and Amstelveen.

BEGINNINGS 1950-1970

HOW IT ALL BEGAN

As a little boy, I walked out of the school building one day when another boy suddenly ran towards me. He threw me to the ground, pulled me by my hair and tried to strangle me. I couldn't breathe and was scared shitless. It was the first time in my life that I encountered violence and it made a deep impression on me. When I came home I told my mother about the incident. She said: "Well, my boy, I think it's time for you to learn some self-defence. You should take up judo."

So thanks to my mother, judo was the first martial art I was exposed to. I started taking lessons under Tonnie Wagenaar in a neighbourhood in Amsterdam called Slotermeer. He hired a hall under the famous Hotel Slotania. Tonnie Wagenaar was the best judo instructor in the neighbourhood, the Dutch judo champion in the heavyweight division. I trained judo from the age of 6 to 12 and eventually made it to the level of brown belt. I couldn't do the exam for black belt because you had to be a certain age. That was a rule back then; I don't know if it still applies. I was pretty good at judo and really enjoyed it. I practised a wide variety of sports in that period: soccer, cycling, athletics. I was always a pretty good runner. I was quite good at soccer too, but because I worked in the catering industry I couldn't train in the evenings or on Sundays, so I was never allowed on the first team. I missed quite a few chances because of my work and it made me more dependent on individual sports.

I was born during the war and we didn't have a lot of money while I was growing up. I was following VGLO [*Voortgezet Lager Onderwijs* – lower vocational education] as a teenager, which was the lowest level but one in the secondary school system. Halfway through the last year I started to work, but the school awarded me my certificate anyway. My first job was working in a storehouse where I was always doing crazy things like squats and push-ups in the back room, which drove my bosses totally mad. My parents had a feeling that I wasn't very happy with this situation and showed me an advert for a job on a cruise ship. I was just 17 but I applied for the job and got it. I had already gained experience in the catering business by helping my father who was manager of a hotel on Damrak called Hotel de Pool, located right across from the Amsterdam Stock Exchange.

LIFE AT SEA

The first ship I worked on was the *Oranjefontein* which went to South Africa. In the beginning we slept six guys in a cabin without air-conditioning. We used to play soccer on land after we arrived in South Africa. It was really a great time and I stayed in the job for almost two years. One of the guys on board was Laurens Kuiper, who was the Dutch boxing champion in the light heavyweight division. We trained together on the deck every evening: jumping rope, shadowboxing, stuff like that. There was also a wrestler who I trained with and a man who knew *savate* (a French form of kickboxing). So it was on a cruise ship that I picked up my bent for cross-training in martial arts.

The *Oranjefontein* could accommodate around 500 passengers and cargo. There was first class and second class travel and I worked in the first-class section. Because of my experience in catering, I was already a salon attendant in first class at the age of 18 and had an assistant who was much older. We would pick up the passengers in Southampton and the first stop after Southampton was Tenerife, in the Canaries. The *Oranjefontein* then sailed to the South African cities of Cape Town, Port Elizabeth, Durban and East London. After that we paid visits to Mozambique and Zanzibar and then back to Amsterdam. The captain was a man that went by the nickname of "Handsome Harry".

When I was 18, I began a relationship with a young woman from the Jordaan [then a working-class neighborhood in Amsterdam] called Joke Koster. However, on one of our trips I got to know a Swiss woman called Ursula Baumann. She was 23 and a classical beauty. She was invited to sit at the captain's table with all the important passengers. One day I gave her a plant, telling her it was "for the most beautiful girl on the boat". That was the beginning of our relationship. Handsome Harry, in his 40s with his uniform and all his insignia and stuff, also seemed to have an eye for this female passenger, but fortunately she preferred me. Her parents lived in Switzerland in Zürich am See as well as in South Africa where they had a farm with a workforce of about 100 people. And this was only more of a hobby, to give you an idea of how rich they were. Her father would ride around on a horse through his fields and only black people would be working the land. This was during the apartheid period when Hendrik Verwoerd was prime minister.

When I went back to Amsterdam I resumed my relationship with Joke and she became pregnant. But the rich lady had said: "Why don't you come with me to South Africa?" She had plane tickets for the whole thing and wanted to meet in Paris. I thought to myself: "Well, I'm not married, so why not?" I still hadn't come to terms with the fact that Joke was pregnant. I packed my bags the next day and went to Paris where I spent the night in a hotel.

I was lying in my hotel bed when it suddenly dawned on me: "I'm such an asshole. I'm lying here waiting for a woman to go to South Africa and I'm leaving a girl behind in Amsterdam who's carrying my child." I lay awake thinking about it the whole night and at 6am the following morning I caught the first train back to Amsterdam. I never said anything to the rich lady who came to Paris the following day with two tickets. By that time I was back in Amsterdam. I never saw her again.

I married Joke and we had two children, a boy and a girl. Our marriage lasted for 12 years, but somehow she wasn't my ideal partner. We married when we were only 18 or 19 and had children when we were barely adults ourselves.

DUEL IN DURBAN

On one occasion we were in Durban for one week with a nice crew. Three or four of us went to a club and we were mingling with the local ladies who seemed quite interested in us. At some point during the evening the staff of the club warned us: "You'd better watch out, guys, if you go outside. There's a group of men waiting there for you." When we left the club there was indeed a group of men waiting for us. One of them was a guy with a pockmarked face who flipped open a stiletto. I managed to get the stiletto from him and stabbed him in his thigh. We slid alongside the walls of the club into the main street when we heard a police car. When the local boys heard the sirens they quickly ran away. The police brought us back to the boat.

One of the guys from this time recently found me through Twitter and dropped by in the gym where I still work out every morning. He recounted the whole thing. To tell you the truth, I had forgotten all about it. He later became a police officer in the Northern District of South Africa. He published several articles online, but never about this incident as it wasn't in keeping with his function as a police officer. When he recounted the entire incident, which could have cost us our lives, it all came back to me.

In Zanzibar we frequented the bars that were filled with black "working girls". I never drank in that period. You always got a drinking allowance from the ship, but I used to sell mine. It was only at the age of 38 that I started drinking a glass of wine now and then. One evening in Zanzibar one of the guys from the boat was waving around big piles of money. I saw him in a bar getting drunk and paying with the cash, while he was socializing with a prostitute whom I saw leering at his money. So I stole the money from his pocket, leaving a few bills in there. The next day he stormed onto the boat, fuming and still a bit confused. I could hear him shouting in the galley: "I've been robbed. All my money's gone. That filthy whore!" I walked up to him – my mates already knew that I had the money – and said: "Look here." I laid a wrinkled pile of money before him. "What's that?" he said in amazement. I said: "You were so drunk. I wanted to take you back to the ship, but you wouldn't come. I did take your money with me, because I already saw that tart leering at it." My being sober saved this guy several months' worth of wages.

MILITARY SERVICE

Back then there was a rule that said that if you had sailed for two years you were exempted from military service. I was just short of two years sailing, so I had to fulfil my obligatory two years of service. I had very much enjoyed the boxing with Laurens Kuiper so I joined the military boxing team. I fought 22 boxing matches of which I won 21 and lost only one. That was in the welterweight, I didn't weigh that much back then, only about 66 kg. I also played soccer at a very high level. I was in a team with Soares from NAC and Verdonk from PSV [Dutch soccer clubs], then well-known professional soccer players. I also did athletics. There was a rule in the army that if you broke a record you got two days' leave. The record for pull-ups was 32 and when I managed to squeeze out 38 I was awarded with two free days. That record of 38 pull-ups stood for quite a long time. I was in demand in the army because people recognized my athletic abilities. I could box, I broke records at shot put, and ran 1500 metres, which is a valued distance in athletics. Like most athletic types I had a great time in the military.

I was an AMX driver. The AMX is a light tank made by the French. They had speed tests in which they dropped things that you had to maneuver through. My hearing was good, my eyes were good and my reaction time was also very good. It was a very demanding unit; we were just below the level of commandos. The commandos sat in the back of the tank while I drove them around.

I was however a bit of a rebel, that was always in my character. One day, we were having dinner in the army canteen and they served us meatballs the size of marbles that were as hard as stone. I was being a bit rowdy with another lad and threw a meatball his way. He threw one back and within five minutes a food fight erupted. 400 men were throwing food at each other and going crazy. There was a corporal who was in charge and he was bombarded with meatballs while he was shouting "Order!" and "Attention!" As a punishment we had to do drills outside. But we made a real mess of the place given the stroppy mood we were all in.

After you had dinner you always had to bring your utensils inside and put them in a rack like you do nowadays at McDonalds. If it was summer we'd eat outside. There was a pool with a fountain in the courtyard. One time we threw all our utensils into the water. Eventually the pool was filled with knives and forks and the water with fish swimming in it overflowed. We were a bunch of guys always taunting authority.

Me and my army mates used to travel from Amsterdam to our barracks in Oirschot, and on Sundays and we would first go to a night club called *Las Vegas*. One day I told my mates: "I've just about had it with the army, I'm going to quit." That night there was an inspection, you either had to be in bed or in uniform. I was standing there with my tie half-done and the officer threw a tantrum. I had to come to report and I told him I wanted to quit, to which he replied: "Well, you can't."

There was a drill with 144 guys the next morning and we all had to stand to attention. I wasn't standing to attention and a very tall sergeant, a horrible character from the south of the Netherlands, screamed his lungs out at me. At a certain point I became so mad that I took a shot at him! They threw me in jail for two weeks for that. When I was released I had to see a psychiatrist. I told him: "I can't stand it anymore." Of course I could stand it, but I was simply bored with the whole thing. So luckily after four weeks I was released from military service. Exactly what I wanted happened, I had said it would be two weeks before they'd kick me out but it was actually four weeks. I was accepted into the military as a S1 (ideal for military service) but was kicked out with a S5 meaning unsuitable for military service due to mental instability. People told me that was terrible as I would never get a job with the government that way and I told them I had no interest in those kinds of jobs anyway.

STUNTMAN

After my military service I did stunt work for two to three years. I did a lot of stunts for Jacques Tati's series *Les Vacances de Monsieur Hulot* ("Mr Hulot's Holidays"). Tati was a French comedian, a very tall man who always dressed in a long coat and hat; I doubled for him loads of times. I also did a lot of stunts for Holland Location, a well-known film company. A man called Hammie de Beukelaar who owned a pub at Korte Nieuwendijk in Amsterdam always instructed us on how to do the stunts, though he would never perform them himself. We had a lot of work and also did many English movies. At some point a union for stuntmen was set up in the United Kingdom which prohibited the use of stuntmen from other countries. Stunting was very amateuristic back then in the Netherlands. If I asked 500 guilders for a dangerous stunt, then there would be some bloke in a pub who said he would do it for only 250. But then you would later see him walking around with an arm in a plaster cast!

We used our brains with our stunt work. We knew what body parts to protect during different stunts. Falling down stairs is one of the most difficult stunts to perform, you really have to know how to do it without injuring yourself. My stunt team was called Stunt Team Six, as there were six of us. We performed a wide range of stunts: fight scenes, horse riding, motor riding and fencing. I received some fencing lessons from Ger Visser, a well-known fencing coach. We wanted to go professional but this just wasn't possible in the Netherlands at that time. In the US you could earn good money as a stuntman. "Judo" Gene LeBell, a good friend of mine and a fabulous wrestler, earned a good living doing stunts for Hollywood movies.

CHAKURIKI 1971-1975

THE BIRTH OF THE CHAKURIKI STYLE

Sometime around 1971 I became a bouncer in the inner city of Amsterdam. I got to know Otto van Ingen, a then well-known weightlifter who introduced me to barbells. Although I was a rather small and frail young man I gained considerable muscle due from the training. If you're a bouncer and you're really big you can often resolve conflicts by talking. I am not that big so I sometimes had to prove myself. A buddy of mine trained kyokushinkai karate under sensei Jan Stapper and said to me one day: "Why don't you come along?"

So I started training under Jan Stapper, himself a student of the famous Jon Bluming, and made it up to orange belt in two months. That was rather quick as you usually had to wait six month or a year before you could test for the next belt. Jan Stapper's dojo was located in Diemen, just south east of Amsterdam. He didn't have his own gym so we trained in a public school building. There were occasions when there was no key for the building so we trained outside. Jan Stapper was a tough teacher for sure.

During my time with Jan Stapper a kyokushinkai tournament was organized in Groningen in the north of the Netherlands. Jan Stapper said to me: "You can take part, but you'll have to join the black belt team." I was only an orange belt, but my spirit was fierce enough to join the team, so I was allowed to wear a black belt for the occasion. Johan Vos was on the same team together with several other famous fighters. I had to fight a guy from Groningen. We were exchanging kicks when I suddenly punched him in the face. I knew it wasn't permitted and I didn't do it on purpose, but it happened in the spur of the moment. This degree of contact wasn't allowed so I was disqualified although I was way ahead on points.

When I came home I started thinking: "I was the better fighter, but I got disqualified. I don't think kyokushinkai is the style for me. Why don't I combine the karate kicks with boxing?" I worked at it at home for several months, researching many fighting styles through books and picking out everything I thought efficient. I combined the traditional kicking and punching from kyokushinkai with English boxing and judo and started teaching it. It wasn't just street fighting but also contained *za-zen* (seated meditation).

In 1971 I had begun instructing the members of my stunt team in my martial arts style, but I hadn't yet come up with a name. I was very much immersed in the oriental martial arts at the time. I had read about a Korean style called cha-rywk or chakuriki in Japanese in books by Mas Oyama, the founder of kyokushinkai karate. It meant "The Hidden Power" or "The Inner Power". I thought as a derivative of kyokushinkai, why don't I call my style chakuriki? There was still a veil of mysticism surrounding the martial arts and chakuriki sounded really good to me. And chakuriki is very similar to Harinck. All the letters can be found in the style's name, you only have to change the "u" into an "n" (but I only discovered that two years later). So I decided to call my style chakuriki. It sounded good and it has power. In January 1972 I founded my own gym. This means I have now been in the fighting business for more than 40 years.

I taught traditional karate, we wore traditional karate gis, but we also trained boxing techniques. I liked boxing because I thought the punching was very good, but boxing lacked the spiritual aspect. Kyokushinkai had the spiritual aspect but didn't emulate total combat. So that's why I started teaching chakuriki. To make the style complete I also added four weapons: bo, nunchaku, sai and manrikigusari. I taught the use of these weapons for quite some time to my students. I tied a black belt around my waist as I was now the teacher of chakuriki. I was after all the founder of my own style. My students wore white belts.

In karate everyone was wearing white uniforms so I decided to make red uniforms to set us apart. There were no red karate uniforms for sale so I bought white ones and let them soak for several hours in a bucket with red dye. After that we had a red karate uniform. I had about eight or nine students at the time. I rented a small room in a shop so we had a place to work out. There was only one punching bag hanging from the ceiling. I also had some barbells lying around. During the same time I worked as a bouncer at a club called the *iT* with a couple of mates from my stunt team. I was married and had two children and I needed the money.

THE EMBLEM

You can see the following things in the Chakuriki emblem: a yellow sun with a bull-terrier with a branch in its jaws that signifies peace. The yellow sun is surrounded by four weapons: nunchaku, sai, bo and manrikigusari. On both sides we find two fists with calluses on the two biggest knuckles. The bull terrier is the most important. Its characteristics are bravery, intelligence, power, skill and speed. The branch in its jaws symbolises its good character. The chakuriki practitioner sees the bull terrier as an example and strives to have the characteristics mentioned above.

ZEN

A summer day some 2,500 years ago. The Buddha (Sanskrit for 'The Awakened One') was about to hold one of his talks. Several dozens of his disciples were waiting for him to start speaking. The Buddha then held up a flower. One of his disciples smiled. He was the only one who understood that words can never replace reality. It is said that this disciple, who was called Kasyappa, became the patriarch of Zen-Japanese for meditation (in Chinese it's called *Ch'an* and in Sanskrit *Dhyana*). This form of Buddhism was later introduced to China by the legendary Bodhidharma (also known as Ta Mo or Daruma Taiishi). He spent nine years in the Shaolin Monastery in the Chinese province of Hunan. As legend has it, he taught the monks martial arts since their physical health was so bad they fell asleep during meditation. Since that time the Shaolin monks use kung fu as a path to enlightenment, a practice that remains to this very day. In China, Zen Buddhism merged with Taoism, a religion native to China. From China it spread to Korea, Japan and other countries. The Japanese form of Zen is the most popular worldwide, though there are schools that trace their lineage to China or Vietnam.

The Zen school of Buddhism places its emphasis on practice instead of scholarly acquisition of knowledge. In Zen monasteries, everything but sleep is considered to be training. Formal training takes place in the form of sitting meditation called *za-zen.*

Zen was adopted by the counterculture of the 1960s and introduced to the masses through Robert Pirsig's bestselling novel *Zen and the Art of Motorcycle Maintenance*. Nowadays, every major city in the world has one or more Zen dojos. Formal Zen training was introduced to the Netherlands by Jan Willem van de Wetering (1931-2008) who spent a year in a Japanese Zen monastery of the *Rinzai*-sect called Daitoku-ji. He wrote an account in three parts about his experiences in Zen in both Dutch and English. Ironically, Van de Wetering is known in the Netherlands for his police novels situated in Amsterdam.

THE *KI* IN CHAKURIKI

Anyone who has ever looked into the spirituality of the Far East has heard of or seen strange and inexplicable feats. Hindu *sadhus* [holy men] walk on coals with their bare feet without getting burned. Buddhist monks lick red hot steel as if it were a lolly and Taoist priests slash their arms with giant blades, but no blood is drawn. Often these feats are attributed to the cultivation of a mysterious energy called *ki* in Japanese, *ch'i* in Chinese and *prana* in Sanskrit. Several martial arts have made it their mainstay to cultivate the internal power known as ch'i or ki. In China the so-called internal arts like tai chi, pa kua and hsing i have the cultivation of ch'i as a goal. In Japan Aikido and several more obscure arts claim to have the ultimate insights into ki.

Ch'i or ki is an important part of chakuriki: the spiritual foundation of the art is essential. In the early days we would sit in *za-zen* [sitting meditation] at the beginning of class and before competition. In the late 1970s I was being photographed while performing a form or *kata* that is called *ibuki-nogare*, a breathing *kata*. It is first performed with agility and then with power. I am totally focused doing that. After the photographer had the photograph developed he said to me: "I don't understand it! There's some kind of haze surrounding your body." He printed the photograph several times but the haze remained. He said: "It's not the photograph and it's not gimmicks. It's the energy that surrounded your body during that moment." If you ask the average MMA coach about ki, you will probably get a shrug in return. But I am a firm believer in ki.

Especially in martial arts the fighting is essentially a restrained form of violence. You could call it a positive form of violence, at least it has the potential to be used positively. There is so much power in it. There must be a philosophy and a mental foundation behind it to balance out the violence. This is firmly the case in chakuriki, unlike other violent sports like western boxing. There are many good trainers and even many more good champions out there. Many of them will be able to teach you all the basic techniques. But since I started in 1972 to my retirement in 2013 I have produced champions continually. I have calculated that I win around 80 per cent of the matches that I coach. I credit this to the chakuriki philosophy in the sense that you draw on a human being's potential powers that enable him to perform certain feats that "normal" people are unable to do. I did more extreme things in the early years. I had a much longer beard and I often meditated.

Some of that was lost when we switched to modern kickboxing. But it formed an important foundation when we fought our first free-fight matches at Dumerniet's events. We wanted to unite mind, body and soul into a single fighting machine that's used for a higher purpose. That's the spiritual aspect of the chakuriki style and it is very important in my opinion.

FREE FIGHTS

We had been training for several months but there were no opportunities for us to compete. I wasn't a member of the karate-Do Bond Nederland (KBN) or the kyokushinkai organisation. In 1972, I don't recall exactly how but I got an invitation from a man from The Hague. His name was Charles Dumerniet and he had founded the IOG [*Internationale Organisatie Gevechtssporten*/International Organisation for Martial arts]. He was organizing tournaments he called "Free-Fights" in which anyone could enter, regardless of style. Kempo, pentjak-silat, karate practitioners, you name it, they could partake. It gave the martial arts that weren't recognized by the sport authorities, such as judo and karate, a chance to compete.

He either called me or I called him, I really can't remember. Anyway, his first tournament was held on 29 May 1973 in The Hague. There were kempo guys in black karate uniforms, pentjak-silat guys in black satin uniforms and red headbands – most of them were Indonesian or Moluccan young men, and there were taekwondo practitioners. All these different styles took part. My students were fighting in red uniforms with white belts. Some of them may have worn a yellow belt. And they were fighting black belts in those tournaments.

I entered the tournament with a team of six or seven young men. To our own amazement we did extremely well, every fighter came first in his category. We continued partaking in these tournaments for about three years. They were held at different locations in the Netherlands: Rijswijk, The Hague, Amsterdam. It didn't matter where it was, we were there.

Some of my students who took part were Ron Kuyt, Robbie Schumann and Gerard Bakker. Robbie Schumann was a young man I got to know as a bouncer. He was all over the nightlife so I took him under my wing. He lived at my house for a while and called himself "Robbie Harinck", although I never officially adopted him. He even had "Robbie Harinck" tattooed on his arm.

Through these tournaments, chakuriki became famous because of our hard fighting style. The fighting didn't only take place in the halls but often also outside. We had quite an extensive fan club and there were times when we had to form a cordon around the women and children on our way to the bus we had hired, because we were attacked by Moluccan young men. Several times the tyres of our cars were punctured.

Around the same time Charles Dumerniet started up his *Samurai* magazine, which was the first real martial arts magazine in the Netherlands. There had been an unofficial magazine before that time that looked like it was printed on toilet paper. The *Samurai* magazine looked better and in turn highlighted the events Dumerniet organized.

The competition was always held on a mat. At the beginning no punching to the head was allowed, but this soon changed. We then fought with small gloves, like punches, and were allowed to punch to the face. They were a bit like the MMA gloves [light punching gloves] used nowadays. They didn't have fingers, it was a full glove. Charles Dumerniet was way ahead of his time in that respect. Our successes started when we were allowed to punch to the face as I had thoroughly drilled all my students in western boxing techniques.

I remember sometimes walking into the changing room and these taekwondo guys were warming up. They could easily kick a hole in the ceiling and were making near vertical side kicks, but they totally lacked boxing skills. Some of my students couldn't kick higher than the knee, but they could box. So the taekwondo guys didn't stand a chance, they were often knocked out. We won about 95 per cent of our matches. It often happened that all of our fighters took first place. So I have to thank Charles Dumerniet, who is no longer with us, as I really owe that man a great deal.

THE CLASH WITH KYOKUSHINKAI

About four months after I had opened my gym, I was hoovering at 9am one day when a young man walked in. I won't tell you his name out of respect as he has since passed away. He was the Dutch kyokushinkai champion. He said: "I'm here on behalf of Jon Bluming. You're illegally wearing a black belt. You must take if off immediately." I told him: "I don't have a black belt in kyokushinkai, this is chakuriki." He answered: "We have decided that it shouldn't be allowed." I said: "OK, just a moment." I switched off the hoover, spun around and delivered a left hook to his chin that would have killed a dinosaur. He immediately dropped to the ground. The aggressiveness seemed to ooze from his pores and I immediately sensed that he had come to teach me a lesson. I had a reputation to uphold which explains the way I reacted. I grabbed him and yelled: "Get out of here." So he left. People knew me as a bouncer and as you can guess, talk of this incident was all over town before you could snap your fingers.

Every Tuesday night we went running barefeet in the streets of Amsterdam, regardless of the weather. This further cemented our reputation in the city. I yelled out: "*Ich, Ni*" and my students would answer: "*San, Chi*" [this is counting to four in Japanese]. Sometimes we would stand still and practise our *katas*. There was still a big kyokushinkai influence in my style. Due to the extreme training and the fact that it could often be observed by outsiders our fame spread rapidly. We were a walking billboard that attracted certain people. It was a bit of a cult, but in the positive sense (though we did wear red robes).

I had been teaching for a few years when I received an invitation from Jan Stapper. He asked me to participate with a team in a kyokushinkai competition in the famous Hotel Krasnapolsky on Dam Square in Amsterdam. I told him: "That's fine". The kyokushinkai style is known for its hard and rugged way of fighting. In these tournaments the lightest fighter of a team would fight the lightest fighter of the other team. Then the lightest fighter of the remaining fighters would fight the next lightest fighter of the other team, and so on. I didn't have that many heavyweights at the time, maybe just one or two. One had a yellow belt and had been training for about two and a half years. Ron Kuyt, my highest ranked pupil, had a green belt. There were two teams from Rotterdam, one from Groningen, one from Limburg and Jan Stapper was also there with his team. And we were there in our red karate uniforms. Chris Dolman was also attending the tournament with Joop de Vries, the owner of Amsterdam's most famous sex club, the Casa Rosso. Joop de Vries was actually Jan Stapper's boss. He had set up the Oyama gym above the *Casa Rosso* for security heavies that patrolled the red light district to train.

Their intention was to humiliate us. Jon Bluming viewed me as a kyokushinkai renegade who had only trained for a few months and then founded his own style. Bluming thought that was off limits. We fought with small gloves and won all our matches until we were in the finals. We lost the finals on a single fight. Our competitor was a light young man and his opponent was 5 or 6 kg heavier than him. It was the team from Amsterdam, with a lot of heavyweights that eventually won the tournament. However, we got a lot of respect for our fighting spirit from Joop de Vries. He remarked: "I've never seen anything like it." He liked my fighters because they were younger and lighter but made up for it with fighting spirit. From that point on Joop de Vries always sponsored the kickboxing events I organized.

After that tournament they left me alone, they had accepted me. Years later Jon Bluming awarded me a 6th degree in kyokushinkai as a sign of respect for my contributions to the martial arts. Usually people have to pay for Bluming's degrees but I refused.

WAKO WORLD CHAMPIONSHIPS

In 1975 I received an invitation for the European Championships in Berlin, Germany that was organised by the WAKO ("World All-Style Karate Organisation"). It was organized by George Bruckner, Mike Anderson and Bill Wallace. The preliminary rounds were held on mats and the finals in a boxing ring. It was held in Deutschlandhalle and 10,000 people had come to witness the finals. Many schools were taking part. More importantly there were many fighters from the US, mostly soldiers who were stationed in Germany at the time. Most of them were pretty good fighters. In the US the karate folks had been developing full-contact, a form of kickboxing with no knees, elbows or kicking to the legs allowed. They used safe-T-kicks [plastic protection wear, worn a bit like a shoe], you put them on your feet and used gloves where your thumb would fit in. This equipment had been developed by taekwondo master Jhoon Rhee in the US where I saw it for the first time. All sorts of styles were present and we were there, of course, in our red uniforms.

I will never forget sitting in za-zen with my fighters in the dressing room. I was speaking to my students and we were truly fired up. Then I heard a voice behind me say: "Cha... ku... ri... ki, what kind of Chinese food is that?" I paid no attention to it. There were, if I remember correctly, four weight categories. I was there with five students, with two students in one of the four weight categories. Every one of my boys made it into the finals and we eventually won first prizes in three weight categories. Afterwards Bill "Superfoot" Wallace came up to me. At the time I didn't even know who he was, let alone that he was the world champion in full-contact karate. The comment in the dressing room had come from him. He said: "Mr. Harinck, can I talk to you for a second?" He apologised for the rude comment he had made and said: "I have never seen guys fight with that kind of spirit." I thought that was very polite of him to come and apologize like that.

We entered history with our three first places at that tournament. Norbert Schiffer was the owner of several martial arts magazines, including *Karaté*. Several of the magazines he founded are still being published. Those were exceptionally well-produced magazines. They provided us with a podium as they featured reviews of the tournament and interviews with my fighters. In that way chakuriki made its breakthrough on the international martial arts scene.

The news about the WAKO tournament had somehow reached Thailand. A few months after the tournament I received an invitation to come to Thailand with a couple of my fighters to fight in the Lumpinee Stadium, one of the two biggest stadiums in the country as far as audience numbers are concerned. They wanted to invite the best fighters from Europe to fight five top muay thai fighters from Thailand [muay thai literally means "Thai boxing" and it is the traditional Thai form of kickboxing using feet, hands, knees and elbows]. We accepted the invitation. We were the top fighters in Europe at the time and I thought we'd show those people in Thailand what we were made of.

Our training was absolutely brutal. We had night training at the seaside in Bloemendaal every week, and afterwards you had to pull huge thorns from your feet from the undergrowth. We all had enormous calluses on our knuckles, as we did a lot of *makiwara* training. We were living in some kind of frenzy. We were obsessed with martial arts night and day, like a ninja or a samurai, but in a positive way. I instilled the values of discipline, not fighting in the streets and helping the weak in society in my students. I formulated the Five Golden Rules of the chakuriki way of life and these were always recited before class.

The five Golden Rules of the chakuriki way of life:

1. We will try to master the chakuriki way of life as well as possible.
2. We pledge loyalty and respect to our teachers.
3. We will refrain from rudeness and violence.
4. We acknowledge an honest and firm brotherhood amongst ourselves.
5. We promise to undergo the hard discipline and training method for the benefit of mind and body that characterizes our style faultless and courteous.

I always said to my boys: "Don't go around looking for fights. Leave the situation if you have to. But if you are forced to fight and cannot avoid it, don't make a half-assed effort." I hold the same values today. I never try to fight, but if I have to... I mean you're a fighter and that doesn't mean that you have to let yourself be bullied. I always tell my students not to fight in the streets. I think it all goes back to the incident I recounted earlier when an older boy I didn't even know pulled a take-down on me and tried to strangle me. Something I myself would have never done to anyone else. I didn't want that to happen ever again. Our style of fighting is very offensive, but the defence is still its core.

THAILAND AND BEYOND

THAILAND

So we got our tickets to Thailand and on arrival were brought to our hotel. For a couple of days we were taken sightseeing. But then we went to the stadium to watch a few matches. It was the first time in my life that I had seen muay thai. I sat down in amazement and thought: "We will never be able to beat these guys." They were using their shins like baseball bats, attacking every part of the body but the groin. Then the clinching, hanging around each other's necks like monkeys anticipating even the slightest push or pull. And then the most fearsome weapon of all: the elbows. They would flick out elbow strikes from every possible angle like the tongue of a venomous snake. We couldn't do all that, nobody had ever taught it to me.

We worked out in the evenings in the scorching heat. That too was new for us. It was the first time we'd gone to fight outside of Europe. I had a good look at muay thai and we trained in some of their techniques the last few days before the fights. But these are skills you can't really learn in just a few days.

The Thai boxers had already fought the top taekwondo fighters from Korea, the best karateka from Japan and the most experienced kung fu fighters from Hong Kong, but these had all been slaughtered. We could kick, we could box and we trained hard. The photographs taken at the time show that my fighters were all in excellent physical shape.

It was total chaos in the stadium in Bangkok. Muay thai was just as popular back then in Thailand as football was in the Netherlands. The press was there, crowds, everyone. Guus de Jong, a reporter from *Panomara*, a well-known Dutch magazine accompanied us.

They might have been a bit cautious as they had seen us train. They pulled all kind of tricks to humiliate us. I couldn't even coach my fighters as there was such a large throng of people around the ring. They didn't care.

The first fight. I don't remember who it was, but my student was knocked out in the first round by an elbow in a bout that was scheduled over five three-minute rounds. Second fight: again my student was knocked out in the first round. Only Ramkisoen, a lightweight of 57 kg, made it to the third round. His weight class is probably the most difficult in muay thai as 57 kg is about the weight of the average Thai male and there is no shortage of competition in this weight category. Becoming a champ in the 57-60 kg weight division in muay thai is comparable to reaching the top of the Himalayas in mountain climbing. He fought the champion of Thailand and got a lot of respect and a thundering applause because he made it to the third round. But then he too was knocked out. Kuyt and Karakus both made it to the second round.

So, in brief, two were knocked out in the first round, two in the second, and one in the third. "Holy Moses", I thought by myself. Of course the ring experience was definitely on their side. Some of those guys had fought between 200 and 300 matches which is not uncommon for Thai fighters. My fighters had only fought two to three matches in a ring. Instead of viewing the experience as a humiliation, it was what they call in Zen Buddhism a moment of *Satori* - a sudden flash of insight. The experience gave me an impulse to further develop the chakuriki style.

We returned home on the tickets they had given us. I stayed in the Netherlands only for a week and then caught a plane straight back. I trained for three months in three different camps: Petchmuangtrad, Kiatsongnoi and Sityodtong which was owned by Mr Yodtong. The legendary muay thai champion Samart Payakaroon also trained at Sityodtong when I was there. I had a gym and a family back home but I just had to learn muay thai. I saw it as a weakness that we had no knowledge of this brutally effective martial art.

The training in Thailand was grueling to the extreme. You had to train in the burning sun. Sityodtong had a school along the river. Dead dogs floated in it and I stood there brushing my teeth. I lost 5 kilos during my stay. The only thing you ate was a little bit of rice with some fish or chicken. And you worked out every day. You were jumping rope in the burning sun with a rope made out of plastic. I had enormous blisters and sores on my hands and under my feet. Luckily they have very effective herbal treatments in Thailand to let these all heal. When I returned home I was fairly proficient in muay thai. I had even learnt to speak the Thai language reasonably well. Back in Amsterdam I started to teach my team what I had learnt in Thailand.

In 1876 Jan Plas, Peter van der Hemel and Jan van Looijen had gone to Japan with the goal to study tai-ki-kenpo [a Japanese offshoot of the Chinese internal martial art hsing i]. They ended up in Kenji Kurosaki's kickboxing club and trained with him and his champions for several months. Back home Jan Plas founded his own school: Mejiro Gym. In Jan Plas' Mejiro Gym they worked a lot with the low-kick, whereas in my gym we were stronger with clinching, knees and elbows. The Japanese were not that keen on these aspects of fighting. In Thailand, muay thai focused on kicking to the body, but I quickly experienced the effectiveness of the low-kick and introduced the technique in my teaching. If the shin connects to the muscles of the upper thigh it's painful for the person who receives the kick. Even a person impervious to physical pain – if such a person should exist – would eventually lose control over his thigh muscles and balance. As a consequence he would be unable to effectively defend himself without an operative foundation.

In those days muay thai in Thailand would consist of up to 80 per cent leg techniques and 20 per cent arm techniques. Nowadays in Thailand they have adapted their way of fighting to contain more boxing, due to the influence of international competition. It's not so much that they weren't any good at boxing. There were several Thai fighters who became champions in both muay thai and western boxing, such as Kaokor and Khaosai Galaxy. These identical Thai twins were the first twins to become world champions in boxing. On the other hand there are camps in Thailand that hardly do any boxing at all; it's just knees and kicks. It varies from camp to camp, with every camp having its own specialty. You saw very dark-skinned Thai fighters in matches in Thailand. They were children of US military personnel who had been stationed in Thailand and had Thai mothers. There was a national champion in Thailand and I don't recall his name, but he was very dark-complexioned.

The Thai boys are super athletes and they are still our superiors when it comes to fighting according to full muay thai rules in the 40 to 60 kg weight categories. They would start living and training at one of the camps around the age of four. Often they were children of poor families. They would stay in the camp as long as they would fight and it was kicking, punching and clinching day in day out. In Europe kids had to go school and learn a profession. The Thai kids would fight their first match at the age of five or six and they would fight for money. They may have earned as little as 10 or 20 Bath, but it was a start. If they won, they'd get a bonus. Half of the earnings would go to the camp. In Thailand, muay thai is one of two avenues for common people to escape poverty, the other being the sex industry.

This arrangement has changed only in the last two decades. Today attending school is compulsory for children in Thailand, but during the time that I was there, they could train all day long. They were incredibly skilled, incredibly fast and incredibly strong. The only drawback was that their weight categories ranged from 40 kg to about 65 kg. Very seldom would they have a champion who exceeded 70 kg.

Changpuek Kiatsongrit was an exception. He eventually ate his way up to 84 kg, but originally he fought in the 70 kg weight class. In the West this situation is reversed. The majority of fighters fight in the 70 kg and upwards weight categories. Almost all western participants in K-1 Max events actually have to diet down to the maximum weight of 70 kg. It's not uncommon for K-1 Max fighters to weigh 5 to 10 kg more than their competition weight in the off season.

When I went to Thailand to train for the first time, I was the only white guy around. People were touching my white skin and the hair on my arms, they had never seen anything like it before. You would sleep with eight other people in a little hut. Nowadays Camp Sityodtong has luxury accommodation. You can take your family with you, they have swimming pools, all rooms have air-conditioning and the restaurant serves delicious Thai food. You pay a lot more for this, but they're always fully booked, all year round. People from every corner of the globe come there to train. There are Swedes, Americans, Australians, you name it. They will have a Thai trainer there, but the boys from abroad will also spar against each other, which improves their skills.

Over the last quarter of a century there has been rapid development worldwide. I did quite a few seminars abroad in the 1980s and 1990s. I would get many international visitors to my school who would then start teaching what they had learned at their own schools. It spread like an oil slick. At present the Netherlands is the number one kickboxing country in the world, but we should be on our guard that the Eastern European countries don't overtake us. Their fighters are getting better and better. They train in Thailand as well as in the Netherlands. In the 1970s Amsterdam was the only destination if you wanted to train kickboxing, but nowadays they can go to Breda or Groningen to receive expert tuition. We all know the techniques, so it doesn't make much of a difference where in the Netherlands you train.

There is a professional organization called *SuperKombat* based in Romania that sets up well-organized events with good fighters. A few years ago a group of Romanians came to my school to help prepare a young man, and you could see them soaking up all the details. They copied everything, like the Japanese did earlier on. When the know-how is combined with motivation in Eastern Europe, the Netherlands will lose its dominance in the world of kickboxing. I predict that in ten years we'll have a totally different situation in which the Eastern European countries will dominate.

RAM MUAY

The *ram muay* [fighting dance] or w*ai kru* is a ritual that always precedes a muay thai match in Thailand. I taught it to my students in case they had to fight in Asia. In Thailand a kickboxing event will host 7 or 8 matches during one evening. In the Netherlands we will have up to 20 fights during the evening. With 20 ram muay performances an event would last twice as long. The spectators in the Netherlands don't have the patience to sit through such a ritual and it's not part of our culture. Besides that, a European won't be able to do it correctly, with the exception of a few fighters like Ryan Simson who have spent extensive periods of time training in Thailand.

If my boys fought in Thailand we would do a ram muay. Each camp in Thailand has its own ram muay. It's a basic dance by which one can recognize to which camp a fighter belongs, with certain individual touches. A fighter might emulate shooting you with bow and arrow or burying you in a grave he's dug. There's a spiritual element involved in the sense that the fighter prays to the spirits and Buddha for a successful match. Most of the Moroccan and Turkish young men that I trained wouldn't take part in a ritual that belongs to another religion. For them there's only Islam.

THE FIRST KICKBOXING EVENT (31 May 1976)

I had heard that there was another gym in Amsterdam called Mejiro Gym and that they practiced a form of kickboxing they had learnt from Kenji Kurosaki in Japan. Mejiro Gym's sensei Jan Plas had founded the NKBB (*Nederlandse Kick Boxing Bond*/Dutch Kickboxing Association) with Jan van Looijen, a very experienced detective in the Amsterdam Police Force, and Peter van den Hemel. All these guys had a kyokushinkai background; I think that Jan Plas was even a 4th or 5th degree black belt. In 1976 Jan Plas walked into my gym in Van Beuningenstraat with his girlfriend, Gerda. I had never met him before. I was training with the competition group around 7pm in the evening. I had somewhere between 100 and 150 students. He said: "I'm organizing a kickboxing event in the Jaap Edenhal [sports hall]. Do you want to take part?" I said: "Sure, that would be great." He explained the rules to me, which included low throws. This was a Japanese tweak of the traditional muay thai rules.

The Netherlands' first kickboxing event was held at the Jaap Edenhal in Amsterdam on the evening of Monday 31 May 1976. Flyers were all over town and the event was completely sold out. There were participants from the Chakuriki gym, the Mejiro Gym and some all-style practitioners. The very first kickboxing match ever held in the country was with my student John de Ruiter who knocked out his opponent John Schreve with an elbow strike in the second round. Most of the other fights were Chakuriki fighters versus Mejiro Gym fighters. Robbie Schumann fought Lucien

Carbin and lost. Johan Vos fought Gerard Bakker who was not a technical fighter but a real Chakuriki fighter with a lot of spirit. Johan Vos received a terrible beating in that match. He was knocked out in the third round by several downward elbows to his head. Eventually we won three of our matches and Mejiro Gym two. Due to the elbows in the match between Gerard Bakker and Johan Vos we had to appear before the mayor of Amsterdam: after that elbows were illegal in Dutch kickboxing matches for a long time. It was not until 1987, when Ivan Hyppolite fought Orlando Wiet at the Jaap Edenhal, that a bout with full muay thai rules was fought again.

Jan Plas' fighters all wore long satin trousers while we wore muay thai shorts. We were often criticized because we were introducing new things all the time, but in retrospect it was fun to be able to witness all these developments firsthand.

People in Amsterdam used to call us "the students" because they thought we were educated simply because we lived in the western, posher part of Amsterdam. I was never a student, although my current spouse lectures at the Free University. The Mejiro Gym fighters were called "the workers" as they all worked in the inner city. They worked at Hotel Torenzicht, the *Casa Rosso* and for Aurore Robert's Chinese restaurant. The rivalry between the two schools became a bit like that between Ajax and Feyenoord [Amsterdam versus Rotterdam] in Dutch football, and provided a very strong impetus for the development of kickboxing in the Netherlands.

The NKBB organized matches for several years, mostly Chakuriki versus Mejiro Gym. A few years later some fighters emerged from Rotterdam. Joop Musterd and Martin Borneman, two taekwondo teachers, had started to teach American full-contact kickboxing. Their students were very good with side-kicks and all those flashy kicking techniques that full-contact is known for. They could hold their own with that to a certain degree, but they had no defense against knees and low-kicks and always got beaten in the end. So for a number of years, Amsterdam was not only the capital of the country but also the capital of Dutch kickboxing.

In the late 1970s I opened an extension of my gym in Utrecht. Kenneth Ramkisoen, one of the fighters who had accompanied me to Thailand, said to me: "There are a lot of eager guys walking around in Utrecht who are not in a position to travel to Amsterdam. Could you teach them?" So I started to teach in De Meren, a large sports centre in Utrecht. The school did very well, at one point I had about 100 students. It was often said in those days that the Amsterdam mentality was the best for becoming a champion. But before we knew it, we had two national champions from Utrecht.

Nowadays there are several thousands of kickboxing gyms all over the Netherlands and there are top fighters from even the tiniest village. I continued to teach in Utrecht for several years and opened another branch in Haarlem around the same time together with Ron Kuyt, who was from there. Dick Vrij was one of the best-known fighters of the branch in Haarlem. He fought for Chakuriki up to the B-Category [fighters in the Netherlands have to work themselves progressively through the N, C, B and A-categories before they fight the full five rounds of three minutes]. Later he started training groundwork under Chris Dolman and became one of the first "Free-Fighters" in the Netherlands [Free-Fight is actually a precursor of MMA or Mixed Martial Arts].

CHAMPIONS IN THE 1980S - PART ONE

IWAN DE RANDAMIE

I had a young man under my guidance called Iwan de Randamie. He was the child of a Dutch mother and a Surinamese father. He was a very sweet, soft kid, still at school. His life revolved around Thai boxing. He was shy, but transformed into an animal in the ring. He became the Dutch champion in the 59 kg category. At some point he got a girlfriend. His parents once told me that the gym was everything for him. His life consisted of the gym, school and later his girlfriend. One night he had taken out his girl for a night on the town and was driving on Admiraal de Ruijterweg in Amsterdam. A drunk driver ran a red light and his car collided with de Randamie's. The latter was unscathed, but the girl was killed instantly. The young man went crazy with grief. Two weeks later he came to me and said: "Sen, I can't live with this. I'm going to shoot that bastard." I said: "Son, you can't do that. You'll have to suffer the consequences and it won't get you your girlfriend back." "OK, then I won't," he replied.

One week later I was driving in my car with Aurore Robert, my girlfriend at the time. We had just come back from Belgium. I suddenly started feeling very uneasy. I told her: "Aurore, I think there's something wrong with my kids." I had two children with my ex-wife. So I called my ex-wife and she said: "No, no. Thommie is here and Petra's out with a friend. It's all good." So I thought: Well, then everything is OK. That evening I was at home and de Randamie's younger brother came to my front door. He was in tears and said: "I have to tell you something." "Well, what's wrong?" I asked. It turned out that de Randamie had gone to the drunk driver's home. He went into his house and told him: "You killed my girlfriend with your drunk driving. My sensei told me I couldn't kill you, but he didn't tell me I couldn't shoot you in your knees." He shot the man in both knees and then shot a bullet through his own head.

He had written a farewell letter that was delivered to me by his brother, in which he wrote: "Sorry, sensei. I followed your advice, but I couldn't live with it. I want that man to suffer. I'm going to shoot him in his knees and use a third bullet for myself. I hope you're not mad at me. *Oesh, sensei.*"

"PLOOSIE"

Around the same time I had another young man in the same weight category as de Randamie. His name was Richard Ploos. His parents had emigrated from Indonesia to the Netherlands. They were so called *Indos* [in Dutch], meaning that they were of mixed Dutch / Indonesian ancestry. Ploos walking would walk with stooped shoulders, looking at the ground, wearing spectacles and carrying a little briefcase. He was a very sweet young man and would never speak unless spoken to.

We went to Paris where Richard had to fight for the European title. We were in the venue and suddenly I couldn't see him around. I thought: Where has that young man gone? I looked around and suddenly saw him sitting higher up in the hall. I didn't say anything about it and later we went out for dinner. The first matches started between 8 and 9 pm. I asked him: "What were you doing up there,

Ploos?" He said: "Sensei, I wanted to be able to see how people would see me during my match." I thought that was quite funny.

He lost his match, a terribly hard match, on points. He had to fight a half-Asian from Paris. Richard was only 18 years old. The spectators were the true winners. One day back in the Netherlands, he went from the gym to his house by public transport. He wore a leather jacket and carried his briefcase while he was waiting for the bus. Three street punks approached him. One of them kicked at his briefcase. After that he held it in front of him. One of the guys shoved him. Then another guy started kicking him. Nobody in their right mind would ever think, with his appearance, that they were messing with a fighter. Suddenly he straightened his back and seemed to transform into a pit bull terrier. He knocked each one of them out with a single punch. This happened after he had tried to avoid the fight for five minutes. His neighbor had seen the whole thing happen and recounted it to me when I ran into him in the cigar shop.

The next time he came to the gym he didn't say anything and headed straight to the dressing room to change. When he came out of the dressing room I said: "Ploos, could you come into my office for a second?" I asked him: "Has anything happened?" "No...No, Sen," he stammered. I said: "Because I heard you got into a fight. Why didn't you tell me?" He replied: "Because I thought you would be mad at me. I thought you told us not to fight in the streets." I replied: "Well, I told you not to go looking for fights, but if you cannot avoid it, then don't make a half-assed effort." He started laughing and said: "Sen, they were calling me names, really insulting me. They kicked my bag. When I had to fight I knocked them all out." I gave him a hug and said: "Son, that's fantastic." That's how it should be; he didn't continue kicking while they were on the ground or anything. He just knocked them out and that was the end of it. After that some people intervened.

A few weeks later Richard was watching a recording of his fight in

France with his mate Danny, whose last name I've forgotten. They were of the same age. At some point his father returned from his work and walked into the living room. Danny later told me the whole story. His father said: "I want to watch tennis. There's tennis on TV." Richard replied: "OK, dad. We just want to watch the last round of this match. Is that OK?" His father walked to a fruit bowl, grabbed a knife and stabbed his own son in the stomach. Richard collapsed. Danny saw the blood gushing from his stomach and ran outside. He was in shock. Richard died in the living room of his own home. His father was arrested and received a prison sentence for murder. Richard's father had been in the internment camps in Indonesia during the Japanese occupation of 1942-1945. This left him with a syndrome and he had acted out during a flashback. Eventually he only served three years in prison.

But this young man was now dead. There was disbelief and shock in the gym. This was number two. Students were saying things like: "Sen, I can't take this. If that guy gets out of the cooler we're going to waste him." This talk went all over town and at one point I had the police in my gym. They said: "Mr Harinck, we need to talk to you. We've heard that students of yours are planning to take revenge on Richard's father." I replied: "I know, but do you think that's strange? That frail, little young man being stabbed to death by his father." The police replied: "We know, but they'll have to suffer the consequences. You must try to suppress it." Later I sat down with my students and said: "Guys, we really can't do this, it would be illegal to take the law into our own hands."

When Ploos' father was released from prison he was given a new identity by the authorities and never lived in Amsterdam again. There were students of mine, kids really, who had sworn on Richard's grave that they would take revenge on his father. So there were two young men, both of them Dutch champions, both of them in the same weight category and both of them were dead within a year. One committed suicide and the other was murdered by his own father. This was probably the saddest thing I encountered in my life as a kickboxing coach.

SASKIA VAN RIJSWIJK

One day in 1974, a streetwise Amsterdam girl named Saskia van Rijswijk entered my gym. During her first class she was chewing gum and answered back at me which was unheard of in my gym. "Don't bother coming back," I told her after class. The next day she was back again and apologized for her behaviour. I had let her spar with some of the advanced girls I was training and Saskia had got quite a beating. She had already made up her mind that she was going to get even with those girls. After three months she was the superior of the girls who had beaten her up during her first lesson. From then on she developed into a rugged fighter who won the world title against a Thai opponent in 1981. "Fear" wasn't a word in her fighting vocabulary. Her endurance was great, though technically she wasn't that gifted. But by biting into a match like a bull terrier she became a reasonably good fighter. It was through my contacts with Carter Wong that she got a leading role in a movie made in Hong Kong.

In Thailand the women are not allowed to fight in the same ring men fight in. This is probably due to an animist belief that predates Buddhism. There has never been a single ladies' match in either the Lumpinee or Rajadamnern stadiums in Bangkok. Women are allowed to train in the camps. The level of the ladies is in no way comparable to that of the men and there are not that many female Thai boxers in Thailand. There is one fighter who I think is very good, who is one of Thailand's many transsexuals. She's actually a woman, but behaves, trains and fights like a man. Her name is Parinya Charoenphol. I was the first to offer separate kickboxing classes for kids and women in the Netherlands. But at the end of the day, I would rather watch men fight than girls or little kids.

In 1996, Lucia Rijker fought against a male Thai opponent who was 5 kg lighter. She was knocked out after 30 seconds in the second round. Johan Vos thought she'd stand a chance. As a coach I personally would never let a woman fight a man. I think that's absurd. It was just an attempt to gain publicity on the part of Johan Vos.

RIK VAN DE VATHORST

Rik van de Vathorst had started training muay thai at the Samurai Gym under Peter Stolp, but switched to my gym after a few years. He wasn't the most technical fighter in the gym, but made up for this with his fighting spirit. He was strong and rough as a fighter, but as a person he was always very polite and well mannered. I always start my classes with rope jumping, an excellent exercise to train endurance and timing. At the start of his first lesson I said to Rik: "We're going to jump rope." And Rick responded: "I don't have a jump rope." I said: "You can use this one," and handed him one. It turned out he couldn't jump rope at all. This was cause for a lot of laughter in the gym. I let him jump rope before each class. It took him ages to master this exercise, but when he finally had it, he was the best rope jumper in the gym.

Rik became Dutch champion under my guidance and his fighting career was going very smoothly. He had to fight in Paris for the European title against Youssef Zenaf, a French champion. This was a match on WKA-kickboxing rules [no knees and elbows, low-kicks allowed]. He had to wear long satin pants and safe-T-kicks. Rik was warming-up in the dressing room and delivered a front kick to the wall in front of him and I heard a loud "Ouch!" echoing through the dressing room. Within minutes there was a lump on his foot the size of an ostrich egg. I was angry as hell and came down in a fury. "You stupid asshole, how could you do that?" If you kick a punch bag it will give way, but a cement wall won't. It was due to his fighting spirit. You have to constantly keep an eye on guys like that, but he was just getting warmed up with some shadowboxing.

I said: "Your fight is off. You can't even stand on that foot." But he said: "No, Sen, I came here to fight, so I'll fight." So we taped his lump and put ice on it to reduce the swelling. We still had half an hour to go until the match. We had to walk quite a distance over the catwalk to the ring. Rik isn't much of a dancer on the catwalk and I said to him: "You mustn't show them you've got a foot injury or we won't fight." "Oesh, Sensei," he replied. He always listened to me. The fight was scheduled over seven two-minute rounds. I said to him: "You won't last the full seven rounds. Knock him out in the first round. Anything goes." His opponent, Youssef Zenaf, was a very technical fighter who could sidestep very well and was an expert in fighting while retreating. I said to Rick: "Finish him." On paper Zenaf seemed the best fighter with the most experience, but Rik knocked him out in the first round. We were all ecstatic. Nobody had expected this. We had to carry Rik back to the dressing room as an injury like that becomes very painful when you stand on the foot.

Rik also knocked out a couple of good Dutch fighters, so I was looking for a Thai opponent for him. The Thai champ Fanta Attapong had defeated WKA world champion André Brilleman. I wanted to set up a fight between Fanta and Rob Kaman. Kaman didn't seem to be very keen on the idea, but he might have had his reasons. I arranged for Rik to fight Fanta instead. It was Fanta's third fight in the Netherlands, he had won the first two times. Rik had gone to Thailand to train for three months together with my son to prepare himself for this match. They went to one of the training camps where I had trained, so he was pretty familiar with the Thai style of fighting.

The event was held on 27 January 1985. Rik had an injury, but we had to go along with the fight as it was the main match. He had hurt his wrist: one glove was much bigger than the other. During the match there was a scuffle and Fanta was on the mat with both knees when Rik delivered two penalties to his head. The rules state that as soon as a hand touches the mat, no techniques may be delivered. But Fanta was hanging in the ropes, with no hand touching the canvas. Rik therefore won against Fanta Attapong on knockout and wasn't disqualified. The guys from Mejiro Gym were all saying that it was an unfair win and I admit that it was a dubious decision. Rik was one of the first Dutch fighters ever to knock out a Thai fighter.

When we left Thailand in 1976 I said: "One day we'll defeat the Thai fighters at their own game." I continued saying this over the years and luckily I was able to realize this dream.

CHAKURIKI GOES GLOBAL - PART ONE

SAVATE

The late Bob Blokziel was the main waiter of restaurant d'Vijff Vlieghen / The Five Flies at Spui in Amsterdam, a restaurant that still exists today. In the early 1970s we weight lifted together. Blokziel was the body-building champion of the Netherlands. Through his culinary contacts he had a lot of friends in France and one of his friends was a champion in savate. Through him I received an invitation to partake in a savate competition. He did say beforehand: "There are certain techniques that are forbidden and certain techniques that are allowed. You'll have to learn them." He gave me a video tape of some savate matches.

I went to France with my top team consisting of Gerard Bakker, Ron Kuyt, Robbie Harinck and John de Ruiter. It was at the Méridien Hotel where the first International Savate Championship was being held. We would fight the champions of France and Europe. France and, to a lesser degree, Belgium were the top countries in savate. We lost three matches and won two. The lightweights and the middleweights were particularly outstanding, we didn't stand a chance against them. They were fabulous boxers and very good kickers. It was a completely different style of kicking. We were used to the "raw" low-kicks with the full weight of the body behind the kick. Savate kicks are flicky in their nature. You are not allowed to make front kicks. There were a lot of side-kicks (I forget the French name for them) that were used to push away an opponent. In those days, the savate people were better ringfighters than the karate people. Savate is a true ringsport.

In France savate is practiced by the elite, and is subsidized by the government. One time I went with a group of street punks from Kinkerbuurt in Amsterdam to France on a bus. They were all young men with leather jackets and the long hair which was customary at the time. Their opponents were upper class, polite French men wearing suits. When we entered the venue we could almost hear all these French people thinking: "What sort of riff raff did he bring along?" The French were outstanding fighters and technically gifted. Savate is a bit like fencing, but with hands and feet. It is an elegant sport. The kicking techniques of those French guys were sublime. But we were respected because of our fighting spirit. After the event they gave me a savate certificate. I was the first foreigner to receive one.

There are two organizations for savate in France. It used to be one organization, but one faction split off due to a conflict about the rules. They wanted to popularize savate. It was only practiced in French speaking countries and former French colonies. The Netherlands was up and coming. Savate has its own salutation, just like kyokushinkai, and its own dress code. The fighters wear shoes and tight fitting suits with long legs. It never outgrew its status as a sport for the elite. Muay thai was rawer and more spectacular and gradually became the most popular ring sport in France. However, there are still some 50,000 practitioners of savate in France.

After me, Johan Vos taught savate and founded a savate organization. He had a French guy who lived in the Netherlands and taught savate classes at his gym. After the French guy returned to France he got a Dutch guy, Mark Holland, to teach. Vos gym continues to offer savate classes at their new location, a stone's throw away from my old gym in Van Hallstraat. Several Dutch fighters won championship titles in savate in the 1980s and early 1990s, including Fred Royers, Lucien Carbin, Peter Teijsse, Ernesto Hoost and Gerard Gordeau. But as the new millennium dawned, it seemed that the interest in this unique art had faded.

THE JET FLIES TO AMSTERDAM (15 JANUARY 1984)

In January 1984, I co-promoted an event with Peter Stolp where Benny "The Jet" Urquidez and his sister, Lilly Rodriguez, fought world title matches. It cost me seven plane tickets to get those Americans over here. It's craziness if you think about it now. Benny asked an enormous amount of money, much more than any Dutch fighter would ever receive in those days. And then he had to bring his manager and several family members along, otherwise he wouldn't come. I took the whole gang to Volendam, an old Dutch fishing village and hotspot for tourists. We shot some pictures of all of us in Volendam folkloric costumes. I also invited them to my home. I lived in the Jordaan back then, a neighborhood in the centre of Amsterdam. The Americans seemed a bit spoiled, they just sat in my home with their coats on, with bored looks on their faces, while I was doing my best to entertain them. I had a long talk with Benny. Later I read an interview with him in a martial arts magazine and he said that he sat in on a couple of my classes and learnt several new techniques that he hadn't seen before. I thought it was kind of him to say that. I later visited the famed Jet Center in LA, but Lilly's 16-year-old son had just been killed by a motorcycle gang, so the atmosphere was very low.

On 15 January 1984, Benny was to fight Ivan Sprang, a student of Johan Vos. Benny had a difficult time in the first few rounds as Sprang started out very well utilizing his low-kicks. Once in the first round, Benny found himself on his knees after a low-kick. In the last two rounds, Sprang made the mistake of trying to beat his opponent at his own game, and had to pay the price. The referee ended the fight in the last round, after Sprang received three eight-counts. Benny is from LA where several of the best boxing gyms in the world are located. It was a tactical mistake to try to outbox Urquidez. Sprang should have stuck to his initial strategy. The same evening Lucia Rijker defeated Lily Rodriquez by knockout in the first round by torpedoing Lilly's front leg with low-kicks. Lucia became a world champion at the tender age of 16.

This event was sold out. Getting those Americans over cost so much money that we either played quits or made a small loss of a few hundred guilders. The fights weren't broadcast and the sponsors were either coffee shops or brothels. Looking back it seems absurd to organize an event like this, but at the time, Benny Urquidez had become the most famous kickboxer on the planet after he was featured in the martial arts documentary *Kings of The Square Ring* along with Toshio Fujiwara and Antonio Inoki (both from Japan).

Through the event I got to know Stuart Sobel, Benny's longtime manager. My friendship with Stuart Sobel was probably the best thing I got from this event. We remain friends to this day. Years later I was in the US with Gilbert Ballantine and a few other fighters. However, the evening before the event a hurricane had raged over the area. Come the event there were 250 spectators in a hall with 10,000 seats. My boys did fight, but the organizer said he couldn't pay us. He wasn't able to as he received no revenue from the event. I insisted that since my boys had fought, they should be paid. Later Stuart Sobel intervened on my behalf and all of my fighters got their prize money.

HONG KONG

In the early 1980s I travelled all over the globe to give seminars and coach fighters. I went to Hong Kong seven times, which at the time was still under British rule. We fought in the Queen Elizabeth stadium, a big stadium in Kowloon. These matches were always

Holland versus Thailand match-ups. The fighters from Hong Kong were not on a level to be competing against the Thai. The local fighters would fight in the supporting program. They trained in some kickboxing-kung fu hybrid and would beat each other senseless, with a total absence of any technique. It was always good fun to watch.

The events in Hong Kong were organized by Carter Wong, a very big and muscular guy for a Chinese. He was also an actor in scores of kung fu movies. He had good contacts in Thailand and brought the champions of the Rajadamnern and Lumpinee stadiums over to Hong Kong. Antoine Druif, Gilbert Ballantine, Tekin Donmez and Bolem Belaini were fighters who competed in these events. They didn't pay us much, about 2,000 dollars a fight. But the stadiums were filled to the brim and we were glad to be able to fight in successful events like these.

At a certain point, the government of Hong Kong wanted to prohibit these events as there were too many injuries. The injuries occurred not so much in our fights against the Thai opponents, though these were extremely hard matches on full muay thai rules, but during the contests between the local fighters. After the event had run seven times, the government of Hong Kong declared that the matches could only continue if the fighters wore headgear, and this resulted in empty stadiums. So it died out, but it was great while it lasted. I've heard that matches without headgear are currently allowed again in Hong Kong. It might be that the level of the fighters has improved, or that they adapted the regulations.

AURORE

As mentioned before, in the early days of kickboxing, the Mejiro Gym fighters were known as "the workers" as they were all supposed to be working class guys from the inner city. The Chakuriki members were known as "the students", because we were from the west of Amsterdam and supposedly more educated.

I was at a kickboxing event in the late 1970s and there was a beautiful Chinese-Indonesian lady in the front row. She had long, black hair and was wearing a lot of gold. She greeted me every time I passed. I asked my boys: "Who's she?" "She's Jan Plas' boss," they answered. Her name was Aurore Robert and she owned all kinds of establishments in the inner city and all the Mejiro Gym fighters like Jan Plas, André Brilleman and Lucien Carbin worked for her as bouncers. I smiled at her and asked whether she was enjoying the matches and she said: "Yeah, they're great." I sensed that she liked me. "We're going to have lunch tomorrow," I said to her without much further ado. "That's fine," she replied. She gave me the address where I could pick her up. She had a big, open car. She liked to be opulent, and was also highly intelligent, she owned all kinds of real estate beside her establishments.

We struck up a relationship and started living together. She had a home in a big building that she owned on Gelderse Kade, in the heart of Amsterdam's Chinatown. One day she said to me: "I've got some business to conduct in Hotel Torenzicht. Could you fetch me afterwards?" That hotel was also owned by Aurore. Hotel Torenzicht was, by the way, the hotel were the famous Dutch musician / artist Herman Brood used to sleep. I parked my car in front of the hotel, walked out and called: "Aurore!" This was the period when there was quite a bit of friction between the Mejiro Gym and Chakuriki Gym. You should have seen the looks on the faces of the Mejiro Gym crew when I came to fetch her. If looks could kill, I wouldn't be telling you this story today. They had said to her: "Aurore, you can get any guy in the world. Why do you have to date him?" I thought it was funny that the boss of the Mejiro clan was my girlfriend. Our relationship lasted several years.

"ANTON HEYBOER"

It all started with Aurore. She was a woman of the world and very open-minded. Then I met a Surinamese girl, Merlin, in a club. She asked me: "Do you have a girlfriend?" and I said: "Yes, I have a girlfriend." It's impossible for me to lie, but she said: "OK, let's do something together." I gave her my address and said: "Drop by some time." I almost forgot about it. I came home one day and Aurore said: "Thom, I've had a visitor." "Who was that?" I asked and named the names of a few of my male friends. Aurore said: "Merlin dropped by." "Holy mackerel!" I exclaimed. I had already told Aurore about the fact that I had got on well with Merlin. Aurore was OK with an open relationship. Later a German girl joined us. Another Dutch girl was the last to join. So for a period I lived with four women in the house of a famous car racer in Zandvoort that had cost 3 million guilders [about 1.5 million euros], close to the sea. It was a big house with a lot of rooms and a swimming pool. The five of us lived there for about six months. People used to call me "Anton Heyboer" after the famous Dutch painter Anton Heyboer (1924-2005) who lived in a commune with four wives.

Roger Paschy invited me to a kickboxing event in Paris that he was promoting and he said to me: "You can bring your girlfriend if you want." I replied: "I want to come, but I'll have to bring the four of them, because that's how many I have." He laughed and said: "I don't believe you." Come fight night I was sitting in the front row with four ladies.

It all ended with me letting them stay in the house in Zandvoort while I slept in a hotel in Amsterdam. I'd totally had it with women for a while. Later me and Saskia van Rijswijk had a relationship, but that ended after a few years, as she wasn't the ideal partner for me.

DIESELNOI

The best Thai boxer I ever saw in action was Dieselnoi (Thai for *Little Diesel*). Dieselnoi was a long and slim guy. He had some heart problems a few years back, but recovered and is still teaching.

He was the kneeing and clinching specialist of the Lumpinee stadium. Dieselnoi was an absolute master in the clinch. Unlike certain other Thai champions, Dieselnoi never fought a boxing match. Boxing wasn't his thing and he didn't use it all that much, he mainly used his kicks and knees. He retired from the sport in the mid 1980s after there were no more opponents left for him to fight.

Samart Payakaroon, the other famous Lumpinee champion from that period, was more famous than Dieselnoi. He was the man with the best *teep* or front-kick in the business. He was the multiple champion of the Lumpinee stadium around 1980. He later turned to boxing and became world champion with the WBC in 1986. After his retirement from the ring he became a famous singer and released three studio albums. Since 2001 he has made regular appearances in movies. Samart fought Gilbert Ballantine on 5 December 1993, the day Samart turned 31. Samart won on points, but it was a close call.

A fight was arranged between Dieselnoi and Samart on my birthday, 22 December, in 1982. I attended the match in the Lumpinee stadium. It was a fabulous match and one of the most important muay thai fights of the 1980s to be held in Thailand. Dieselnoi weighed a little more than Samart, they were not of the same weight category. For this fight Dieselnoi slimmed down a bit and Samart became a bit heavier. Both of them were champions and icons of Thailand. Dieselnoi won that match, although they had fought each other once earlier and then Samart had won. I have a painting hanging in my home that was made from a photograph of this match. At least, it was presented to me a painting of the match between Samart and Dieselnoi.

FAMOUS FRIENDS

I have no affinity at all with martial arts movies; neither with Bruce Lee nor with later stars like Sylvester Stallone or Jean-Claude van Damme. I didn't watch them at the time and I don't watch them now. Many students got inspired or stay inspired to train by watching martial arts movies, but personally I've never enjoyed them. Of course I heard a lot of students in the gym mentioning

Bruce Lee and even Branko Cikatiç was inspired to start training martial arts by seeing Bruce Lee on the big screen. I know, it's a bit odd. Maybe it's because it's all choreographed and it's not a real fight, so it's something from a fantasy world. That's probably also the reason you won't find me at ringside when my students fight choreographed wrestling matches. I'm above that, I don't do that, out of principle. Peter Aerts has a contract under Antonio Inoki and goes to Japan four times a year to fight choreographed matches. He makes a lot of money that way, but it's not my cup of tea.

Stuart Sobel introduced me to Bob Wall, who starred alongside Bruce Lee in *Enter the Dragon*. Of course I had never seen the movie but others had told me about it. We became good friends. He became a real estate agent after his martial arts career and a very wealthy one at that. He always invited me over when I was in the US. He also came to the Netherlands once with his daughters and we dined together. The last thing I heard about him is that he went totally bankrupt due to the credit crisis.

Gene LeBell is also a good friend. I visited him in his home in California. He has an amazing collection of motorbikes. We rode together and he remarked that I was the only one who could ever keep up with him. I really enjoyed the wildlife where he lived. You could see wild bears roaming the woods from the road.

I also met Chuck Norris a couple of times. He's a really friendly guy and we get along fine. People often used to remark in the past that I look like Chuck Norris. I myself never saw the resemblance, but I heard it quite often. So Bob Wall, Chuck Norris and Gene LeBell are my friends in the movie industry.

I also know Chris Penn, brother of the famous actor and director Sean Penn. He was the coach of the American kickboxing team in the 1980s and was himself an actor of some renown. I got along well with him. He passed away in 2006 after snorting himself to oblivion. He already had that habit in the 1980s. He came over to the Netherlands on one occasion and we went to one of

Amsterdam's most famous nightclubs, the *iT* on Rembrandtplein. He performed the dance that he had to learn for the movie *Footloose*. There was a crowd of people around him on the dance floor. He was pissed and I suspect he also used a bit of something. People were thinking: What a star, what an incredible dancer. But it was all choreographed dancing from the movie. That was an unforgettable experience.

Not only have I met many celebrities from abroad, I've trained a few Dutch celebrities as well. Peter Faber is a Dutch actor with accolades in theatre, TV-series and movies. I trained him in the early 1990s and I found him to be very spirited. We got into contact when I had to teach him stunt and fighting techniques for some movie. Both his sons, Jasper and Daan, have trained in my gym, with Daan even fighting a match in the ring.

THE FRENCH CONNECTION

There are many Vietnamese in France, Vietnam being a former French colony [1887-1954]. Roger Paschy was a well-known fighter from France, who was originally from Vietnam. Later there was Patrick Brizon, a pupil of Paschy, and at some point pupils of Brizon opened schools of their own. An example is René Desjardins, who lost on points against Tekin Donmez for the European title. Paris and Clermont-Ferrand were the two strongest cities in France as far as kickboxing was concerned. In the 1970s it was mostly the Dutchmen who would fight the Thai boxers in Paris. The French weren't at the level yet to be competing against the Thai fighters. I often refereed these matches. In fact, I was the first official referee in France. The know-how of how to professionally referee a match was also something the French still had to learn at that point. You can look up old issues of *Karaté* magazine and you'll see many pictures of me as a referee. And of course there are many pictures of my boys fighting Thai champions like Fanta Attapong and Fadeng in Paris. Technically, the French may even have had an advantage, with the large oriental community, but we were more successful due to our fighting spirit. The French often said: "The Dutch are brawlers." But it was more a consequence of the teaching system than something in our DNA.

England developed at a later stage. It must have been about ten years after we started with muay thai in the Netherlands that the English had some good fighters who were trained by Master Sken or Master Toddy, two Thai trainers who had relocated to the United Kingdom.

I went to France for a European title contest with Perry Ramkisoen from Utrecht. He was a nephew of Kenneth Ramkisoen, who was in the team when I went to Thailand for the first time. He was a Dutch champion in the 75 kg category and an outstanding athlete. The event was held in one of the rougher areas of Paris. At the time, France had a couple of pretty good young men in that weight category, most of them half-Vietnamese. I don't recall the name of his opponent, but the match was a total thriller and Ramkisoen lost on points. I had a briefcase with me that I put under my chair.

After Ramkisoen's match one of my boys suddenly saw the briefcase sliding backwards. He said: "Sen, they're trying to steal your briefcase." I managed to grab the briefcase. Then suddenly the people behind us pulled out spray cans and started spraying us. They were Algerians who were running all sorts of illegal things in the slums. I was able to duck the spray and landed a good punch on one of them. A fight erupted. They kept on spraying and some of my boys got spray in their eyes. We were there with a group of 15-20 guys. It became a massive free-for-all. Eventually it got sorted out. I had managed to get my briefcase back, but some of the boys had got a lot of spray in their eyes.

After the event was finished, we went back to our cars. We had come in five cars. Guess what? All the windows of the cars with a Dutch license plate had been smashed in. Luckily they didn't puncture our tires, but that did happen at another event in France. That night we had to ride back to Amsterdam. Usually that's a trip of six hours. It was a very misty night and it was also pretty cold. We couldn't drive faster than 30 or 40 kilometres an hour. We drove in a line, but of course we lost each other in no time. I finally made it back to Amsterdam. I received a phone call the next day, and it turned out one of my students was in a hospital in Belgium. Because of the mist they had ridden into a ditch. It was Gerold Piqué, a Dutch champion, originally from Surinam. Gerold was a great fighter with a head-turning physique. Due to the accident he lost an eye. Those assholes in France handicapped one of my fighters for the rest of his life. Gerold continued to fight and fought several matches for the Chakuriki Gym after the accident.

CHAMPIONS IN THE 1980S - PART TWO

STUART BALLANTINE

Stuart Ballantine fought in Paris against Dida Diafat. This was a match for the European title. Of course the Chakuriki name was well known in France, but very few of the French had heard about Stuart as a fighter. Stuart, Gilbert's younger brother, had had poliomyelitis as a child. He had a very thin arm and leg on the left side. Yet he made it into the A-category and had some spectacular wins on knockout.

We arrived in Paris for the weighing. The promoter of the event was Sami Kebchi. At the weighing Dida Diafat refused to step onto the scales. I said: "If he doesn't weigh in there won't be a fight." And they said: "Yes, but we weighed him yesterday and he was of the correct weight." I said: "Who cares, let him step on the scales today." But Diafat still refused. So I declared that there would be no match. But Stuart was thinking of his prize money and he had, of course, trained for this match. He said: "Sen, I want to fight. Let's go ahead with it." So I said: "OK, we'll go along with the fight, but under protest." This just isn't fair play and a good promoter should never allow behavior like this.

The night of the fight, Stuart got quite a beating in the first round and received an eight count. But he had fighting spirit, nothing could get him out of that ring. The second round was again for Dida Diafat. In the third round, Diafat couldn't knock Stuart out and seemed to become tired, while Stuart was just getting warmed up. The public could clearly see that there was a partly handicapped fighter in the ring. He might have had a weak right arm, but his left arm was twice as strong and many an opponents had been knocked down by it. The same happened to Dida Diafat in round three, when he got an eight count. Fourth round and again an eight count for Diafat. In the fifth round Stuart knocked him out stone cold. This was a match I'll never forget.

Stuart fought against Hungary's best fighter in Budapest. The general level in muay thai in Hungary was not very high at the time, but they had this young man who was a decent fighter. Come fight night, I was standing in the corner of the ring with Stuart waiting for his opponent to make his way to the ring. It started with a monotone drone as music. Boom. Boom. Boom. Then I saw a group of guys carrying a coffin and waving flags with swastikas on them. I couldn't believe my eyes. The extreme right wing has a huge following in Eastern Europe and apparently some followers had gotten involved in kickboxing. I said to Stuart: "Look at that bunch of freaks. Destroy him." You can guess what happened. Stuart was so aggressive that he knocked him out with a single punch in the first round. This happened when his opponent came in, it was like two vehicles colliding and that usually means a heavy knockout. Stuart's opponent was totally out of this world and could take his right-wing views with him to the land of dreams that evening.

GILBERT BALLANTINE VS RICHARD NAM (7 DECEMBER 1985)

Gilbert was a very technical fighter. He came to me in 1986. He developed and became well known globally. I've been all over the world with Gilbert: Hong Kong, Thailand, Puerto Rico, New York, Canada and Australia. He fought under all the kickboxing rules you could imagine: muay thai, kickboxing with low-kicks, American full-contact and savate.

One fight that stands out clearly in my mind was in Basse-Terre, Guadalupe, an island close to the Antilles. Gilbert fought Richard Nam, France's very best fighter at that time. In the first round it seemed the fighters matched. After the second round, Gilbert said to me: "Sen, I have to stop. He kicked against my knee." When I glanced downwards I saw that his knee was twice its normal size. If Gilbert said he wanted to stop, it must have been something serious, because fighting spirit is his middle name. I grabbed him and said: "If you have the gall to stop, I'm going to punch your head off in the dressing room. We never quit in the chakuriki style. You may get knocked down, but you continue. If you want a short fight, knock him out." It was: "Oesh, Sensei." They do look up to you. He fought an exciting match which he won on points. Afterwards he was beside himself with joy. He said: "If you hadn't pushed me I would have stopped. With another coach I would have quit." This proves the importance of the coach during a fight.

CIKATIĆ VERSUS WILSON (12 SEPTEMBER 1987, FLORIDA, USA)

We received an invitation from a kickboxing organization called *KICK* for Branko Cikatić to fight Don "The Dragon" Wilson at 83 kg. This was one year after the movie *Rocky III* had run in the theaters. In the most successful part of the series Rocky Balboa (Sylvester Stallone,) pits his boxing skill against the Russian Drago, played by Dolph Lundgren. Lundgren was a former European kyokushinkai champion. With this fight they wanted to reenact the fight from the movie: the Americans versus the Soviets, the good guys versus the bad guys. And Branko is that kind of type, a bit gruff while his love for weight training endowed him with the corresponding physique. The Americans on the other hand are more jovial.

In March of the same year Fred Royers, a former WKA-kickboxing champion and coach from the Netherlands, had authored an article for *Karate/Kung Fu Illustrated*, one of America's most popular martial arts magazines. The article was entitled "Why American Kickboxers Can't Fight" and Royers explained in text and pictures why the low-kick was such a formidable weapon. That might have hurt the American pride a bit, but that was the least of our worries.

It was agreed with the promoter that the fight would be held at 83 kg. That was do-able: Branko's normal weight was about 86 kg and it was no problem to get those 3 kilos off. In those days, people didn't really work with contracts in which everything was put down in ink. When we arrived, they said that the fight would be held at 81 kg. I agreed as we were there a week beforehand. We put Branko on a strict diet and had him train hard, but getting those last two kilos off weakened him severely. As soon as a fighter gets into the single digit body fat range there is an inverse relationship, not only in the ability to perform in the ring, but also in the ability to take a punch or kick. Branko was already completely shredded when we stepped into the airplane. Come fight day he weighed 81 kg. Then they suddenly changed the rules. There would be no knees allowed, which wasn't in our initial agreement.

We were warming up for the fight in the dressing room and we had a few Croatians come along, as Branko is originally from there. I had just taped his hands and I had to go to the toilet. When I came back, walking through the corridor, I heard Branko's voice coming from one of the dressing rooms. I walked inside and discovered to my amazement that I had walked into Don Wilson's dressing room. And I was hearing Branko's voice coming out of a microphone hanging from the ceiling! I came down in a fury: "You fucking bastards, do you have to win like this?" Of course I give a fighter a pep talk before the fight, but we also review the strategy we'll be following. They all jumped like startled horses. I said: "Remove that microphone, or there will be no fight tonight." Some guy came to remove the microphone and we got another dressing room.

When we made our way to the ring, all those Yanks were going crazy. They all thought they were in one of the *Rocky* movies. During Don Wilson's entrance to the ring, Bruce Springsteen was there with his guitar to play his song *Born in the USA* live. I later got to chat with Springsteen, who was then at the height of his musical career.

The fight started out good. At one point, Branko scored a low-kick that left Wilson lying on the canvas with a painful look on his face. The referee counted from one to eight. Then suddenly he said "illegal blow to the knee". I had never encountered this before. A low-kick is aimed at the thigh of the opponent – it may connect to the knee – but a match is never stopped when this happens. This would happen with a blow to the back of the head, but not a low-kick to the knee. This was just total bullshit. The referee brought a doctor into the ring. All this went on for about a minute. In every other country the match would have ended. You are also not allowed to touch the ropes as a coach or you get minus points. At one point I yelled at the referee: "Hey, referee, what's this? This fight is over." "You just shut up," was the answer I got. At that time I didn't have the experience I have today. Now I would have flipped open the regulations and held it in front of one of the jury member's nose.

So the referee let the match continue, with both fighters standing their ground, until the fifth round. In the fifth round Branko took a body shot and went down. The referee counted him out. He was completely paralyzed. With all the slimming down, Branko had been reduced to a shadow of his true capacity. Don Wilson won the match. Branko was paid 30,000 dollars for this fight and Wilson 60,000. Besides the prize money Wilson was left with two broken hands. I must add that Don Wilson is a great guy and I respect him deeply. Later he apologized for what had happened and was very sympathetic. He said many positive things about us afterwards. We've remained in contact until today.

GILBERT BALLANTINE VS MILO EL GEUBLI (27 FEBRUARY 1988)

Gilbert's breakthrough match was against Milo el Geubli. El Geubli was seen as the champion in the lightweight division. Earlier he had beaten several famous Thai fighters and won the world championship title of the WKA by defeating Britain's Howard Brown. When both fighters came up to the ring, spectators could clearly see Gilbert sporting an upper body that most fitness models would kill for, while the fat around Milo's waistline indicated that he had been training at the local MacDonald's. In the first round Milo had already been lying on the canvas five times. Gilbert's wado-ryu karate background with its evasive footwork was a definite plus. In the third round, a left hook from Gilbert ended the match and also Milo el Geubli's career as a fighter.

GILBERT BALLANTINE VS STEVE DEMENUCK (21 APRIL 1989)

A few years later Gilbert got a chance to fight for the "Intercontinental Title" of the FFKA-organization. His opponent was an American called Steve Demenuck, a tall, skinny guy. It was a match over 12 rounds of 2 minutes each with full-contact rules. In the first round, Gilbert went down on a spinning back fist, a technique that is outlawed in most forms of kickboxing, though not in full-contact. By count eight, Gilbert was standing, though still a bit dizzy. Hardly five seconds passed and his opponent made another spinning back fist, this time with the other hand. Again Gilbert got an eight count. I thought to myself: "This match is over." By the eight count, Gilbert was standing again and was saved by the bell. Back in the corner I threw a bucket of cold water over his head and asked if he was OK. Gilbert wanted to continue. The first five rounds were for his opponent, but Gilbert became stronger and stronger every round. After twelve rounds, Demenuck was declared winner of the match on points, but Gilbert received a beautiful belt. It was a tight call.

Then something happened that I will never forget. We were sitting in the dressing room and Gilbert asked: "Sen, when do we fight?" I replied: "When do we fight? You've already fought! Look at the belt you've won." He embraced me out of joy. Apparently he'd had a blackout. He fought 12 rounds on the automatic pilot in a sort of trance. Through the immense hard training you can let your body take over. That's why I called my style "The Hidden Strength", because there is strength deep down inside of us that enables us to perform superhuman feats in extraordinary situations.

TEKIN DONMEZ

Tekin Donmez weighed around 57 kg, he fought in the featherweight division. He was the best fighter I ever had. He was a very complete fighter who could do everything: he could hit as hard as a middleweight and kick high and fast. But above all, he had a fighter's heart. I've known him since he was four years old and lived right across from the gym. He was the same age as my son Thommie; they became friends and played together and he came to stay at our house. His parents were immigrants from Turkey who couldn't afford to pay for training, so I let him train for free. It's a pity he never fought Ramon Dekkers, but Ramon was slightly heavier and Ramon had his best years after Tekin was at his peak. Tekin fought with me at his side over the whole globe. He fought many matches against Thai opponents in the US, in LA, Orlando and other cities. The weight category in which he became world champion is around 57 kg. This is the weight of the average Thai male, so becoming a world champion in that weight category is, as mentioned earlier, comparable to climbing the Mount Everest in mountain climbing.

Sadly, he became a drug addict after his career as a kickboxer. He went to Turkey to a special center to rehab many a time. Then he would be OK for a few months, come back to Amsterdam and then start using drugs again. The last time I saw him was on Zeedijk in Amsterdam. I was driving in my car and yelled through the window: "Hey, Tekin!" His face was covered in a rash; he was very thin and pale. I went to park my car and when I was back at the spot where I saw him, he had run away. He didn't dare come eye to eye with me. I was very saddened by this, and have no explanation for it. You see a little boy that comes to sleep at your house develop into a world-class athlete. Later, he degenerates into a drug addict. It hurts me every time I think of it. He was a little guy, but good looking and a hit with the ladies in the Amsterdam nightlife. His parents started out poor but worked themselves up. One brother joined the police, his other brother had a sewing shop and became very rich.

KENNETH PLAK

Kenneth Plak trained at the Samurai Gym before he came to me. He was a very technical fighter. He was KO'd by Branko Cikatić in the 86 kg category in the early 1990s. It must have been after 1995 that he came to me. I got an offer for him to fight an Englishman in Moscow in the middle of winter. The event was organized by three brothers. All three of them wore long coats, like true Russian mobsters. We got a pile of rubels pressed into our hands even before we reached the hotel. We could eat and drink all we wanted, but we couldn't buy any appliances because they were already charging dollars for those. If you wanted to buy a vacuum cleaner you'd have to pay in dollars. We were staying in a luxurious hotel and Gilbert Ballantine had come with me as corner man.

Plak was fighting the main match of the evening. We still had 60 to 90 minutes until the fight. At one point Plak approached me and said in his soft voice: "Sensei, could you get me psyched up a bit and warmed up a bit?" I replied: "It's a bit early, but if you want to, I'll do it." So I let him kick a bit, punch a bit and talked to him. It's very important to talk to a fighter to get him mentally ready for the match. "You'll win, you're going to take that belt." Stuff like that. He was shadowboxing a bit, but suddenly went totally berserk. He punched the mirror in the dressing room to pieces, he kicked over the table and flung himself at me. I asked Gilbert for help and all of us had to hold him back. I gave him a few slaps in his face and said: "Kenneth, it's me, your sensei." When he came back to his senses he said: "Oh, sensei, sorry sensei". His foot was bleeding and there was glass all over the dressing room. We cleaned up, we gave him some water and let him sit down for a bit. "What were you doing?" I asked. "You ask me to psyche you up, but this is taking things too far." He really felt bad about it, he was almost crying. It wasn't really his fault, I understand that. Luckily I was pretty fast and strong at that time, otherwise he would have beaten me to pulp. By the time he was calmed down we had about 20 minutes until the fight. I was afraid of warming him up again, but I said to him: "Forget what happened, focus on your opponent." He won the fight and became world champion. He was awarded the heaviest belt I have ever held in my hands. It was inches thick and made out of steel. A beautiful belt, weighing about 25 kg.

Nowadays, Kenneth Plak lives in Heerhugowaard in the north of the Netherlands. He has a girlfriend and children. He's the only black guy in the whole village. I ran into him at a camping site in Heerhugowaard a few years ago.

CHAKURIKI GOES GLOBAL -
PART TWO

MUAY THAI MAYHEM (9 JUNE 1989)

We went to the US about six times to fight in different locations. There was a period when muay thai was becoming quite popular in the US. We were often asked to compete there against Thai fighters. On 9 June 1989 in Los Angeles Antoine Druif fought Fadeng, the champion of Thailand at the time. Antoine Druif won that match in a full stadium. Rod Kei, a student of Benny Urquidez, was to fight a top Thai opponent called Saekson Janjira. Half of the people present in the hall were Thai and the other half were Americans. Chuck Norris, Bob Wall, Gene LeBell and Jean-Claude van Damme were all present at ringside as special guests. Rod Kei had won the first round quite convincingly, but the Thai fighter started to fight much better in the second round. It's not uncommon for Thai fighters to use the first round just to feel out their opponent.

In the third round, the Thai put on a headlock, which is illegal. Now while the referee was trying to separate the two, with Kei on his knees, the Thai delivered not one, but two illegal knees. One to the chest and one to the head. People were grumbling with displeasure in the hall, I could hear it. The top judge demanded that the referee disqualify the Thai fighter, but the Thai referee wanted to let the match continue. Then all the trainers and helpers jumped into the ring. Somebody threw a chair into the ring and within minutes there was total mayhem in the hall.

I had three boys in that event and I was carrying the bag with all of the fighter's prize money and our passports. I was holding on to it tightly in the middle of a free for all. All the celebrities at ringside dived under the ring to avoid the chairs flying through the air. The security guys, all of them king-sized bodybuilders, ran out of the venue as the Thai were in a fighting frenzy. One of the referees, a guy from Suriname, was hit on the head by a few chairs and was bleeding heavily.

At one point I picked up the announcer's microphone and said: "What are you doing? This is muay thai. This is an honest sport. We fight inside of the ring and not outside it. Gentlemen, please! There are a lot of ladies here. We are sportsmen, not street fighters. Thank you!" And suddenly all became quiet in the hall. They even gave me a round of applause! But as soon as I let the microphone drop the brawling continued just as before, there was simply no stopping it. It was one big mess and shots were even fired. America's biggest news network CNN aired an item about this event. After this, event fights with full muay thai rules were outlawed in the state of California and have only recently been reinstated.

MEXICO

We were invited by a Mexican promoter to fight at three events in his country. The Mexican guy had several schools in different locations in Mexico. He had developed his own style along the same lines that I had earlier in the 1970s. We were there for ten days and three events. They didn't pay us all that much for the fights but they made it all-inclusive. This meant that they paid for the journey, the hotels and the food. That appealed to us. Remember this was before kickboxing became a truly professional sport with the advent of the K-1 in the 1990s. Patrik Eriksson went along,

Bolem Beilani, Tekin Donmez, Bayram Colak and another chap whose name I don't recall. So we travelled to Mexico. Now Americans tend to regard the Mexicans as a bunch of crooks and I know there's some serious stuff going on there currently with the drug wars. But I have to say that I have never met such friendly people in my life. Mexico is a beautiful country and we devoured the chicken and potato chips the Mexicans would cook for us.

The matches were with no knees and no elbows, but kicking to the legs was allowed. The promoter's fighters had won all their matches so far. They had previously invited German and English fighters and defeated them. So we fought six matches against his fighters in every location. The first time in Xalapa we won all six, all by knockout. Then we went to the next place by car after four days. I was allowed to drive several times and really enjoyed touring Mexico. Again we fought six matches. This time we won five and one match was a draw. And that draw was a tight decision, to say the least. Three of the Mexican guys were knocked out. Then we went to Mexico City where we would fight his own students, as the two other places were only branches of his main school. The organizer was becoming very anxious. This time we won five matches and lost one. One of his boys, a lightweight of 60 kg, won his match. That young man was a good fighter with excellent boxing skills. So the organizer kind of lost face as we were also accompanied by a journalist who reported on everything.

I later understood that the promoter was actually planning to do those Chakuriki guys in. He had heard a lot about us. But they had lost all their matches but one. What happened to me in Thailand was now happening to him, but in his own country. I wasn't all that happy with the competition. You always need a good opponent to bring out the best in your own fighter. The Mexicans were very wild. They did have good boxing skills, I have to hand them that. Mexicans are overall pretty good boxers, but they had no idea how to defend against our low-kicks. They had gained most of their experience in the American full-contact circuit. As far as kicking to the legs was concerned, we were lightyears ahead of them. I think one or two of my fighters scored knockouts with punches, but all the other knockouts were due to our low-kicks. The low-kick is a very effective weapon, especially against opponents that don't know how to handle them.

I also gave a seminar that was perfectly organized in a beautiful sports hall. About 60 young men participated. The mayor and the Minister of Sports were there in person to hand me a certificate. The exciting conclusion, however, came the day before we left. We had been in Mexico for three weeks. That night the matches were to be shown on national television. The organizer had sold the rights to the broadcast, that's how he got the money for the whole thing. We were supposed to watch the broadcast in our hotel. The quality of the hotel was not comparable to the hotels you stay in when you fight in Japan, but everything was clean and tidy.

We were all sitting in front of the television set and around eight o'clock in the evening the broadcast started. I could recognize the words "Chakuriki" and "Thom Harinck" spoken by the presenter. We had been to the studio beforehand for interviews. I had an instructional tape out at the time on VHS called *Born to Fight*. They had scheduled an hour to show highlights from the matches. But instead of matches I saw my own instructional tape on national television. I thought, this is probably an introduction and they'll be broadcasting the matches in a few minutes. But half an hour later they were still showing the tape. So I asked the organizer: "What's this?" He answered: "I don't know."

In the end they broadcast my instructional tape in its entirety with some flashes of other sports, because they thought it was a shame that all the Mexican fighters but one had lost. Initially I felt a bit sorry for my boys, but later we had a good laugh about it. The Mexicans have their own form of chauvinism, just like the Americans do. The next day we left for the Netherlands. The promoter told me he'd keep in touch, but I never heard from him again.

THE DEATH MARCH (OHIO, USA)

Gerard Finot, a rather small Frenchman, was a third degree black belt in kyokushinkai karate and a champion in kyokushinkai karate. His father was a doctor in Marseille, also of small stature. He spoke fluent Arabic, which he had learned from one of his girlfriends. He worked as a bodyguard for a certain prince from Saudi Arabia. He showed me a gold Rolex once, a present from the prince he protected. He had all kinds of connections. He got into contact with me when he was living in LA. He always had big plans and, as I later discovered, a lively fantasy as well. Finot had trained in muay thai in Paris under the tutelage of Pudpadnoy Woarawoot, a five-time muay thai champion of Thailand who had emigrated to France in 1979 to teach there. He walked into my gym one day and said: "I'm planning on setting up an American muay thai organization, could you teach a seminar for me?" Of course I agreed. I'm happy to teach anywhere in the world.

So I went by plane to Cleveland, Ohio, where the seminar was to take place. The location was an incredibly large gym that was owned by an enormously rich Italian family. Of course they were gangsters to the core. They were no saints but treated me very kindly. In that period there was a problem between Thierry Verstraete, the chairman of the French muay thai organization, and the organization in the Netherlands. Verstraete wanted to promote muay thai events in the US and there was a lot of money to be made. He wanted to have the exclusive rights on the muay thai competition in the US. Because Gerard Finot got along well with me, he wanted to set up an event with Dutch and French fighters who were not part of the organization. Thierry Verstraete said: "No, that's not allowed. That Thom Harinck guy is not allowed to do that. It should take place under my supervision."

But Gerard Finot had concocted one of his plans. He had said to

Verstraete: "Come visit us over here in the US, I'll pay for your ticket. You'll have to advance the money yourself. We can split the television rights 50-50." I was there at the same time to teach my seminar. Finot wanted to involve me with the organization he was aiming to set up because I was chairman of the WMTA (World Muay Thai Association), the organization I had founded in 1984.

Both me and Verstraete were put up in an excellent hotel. One night we went to dinner with the whole group. I got the impression that that guy Finot had been reading too many mafia novels. We went to an exquisite Italian restaurant in the Italian neighborhood of town. In those days an Italian neighborhood in the US meant only Italian Americans lived there and the melting pot seemed far away. In fact, regular Americans wouldn't even visit the neighborhood and neither did any Afro-Americans. I was told: "No *tootjoune* will enter here" and I didn't know what they were talking about. The Italians called Afro-Americans "*tootjounes*". There was always a guy sitting in the neighborhood church with a machine gun in his hands to make sure no "*tootjoune*" entered the church. This might seem unbelievable, but I saw it with my own eyes. You can hardly imagine what weird stuff I encountered over there.

We were dining around a round table and a small band was playing live music. I was sitting next to Calendra, head of the clan and 83 years old. Some Italians joined us, all in expensive suits. At one point during the dinner the band approached us and started to play a certain song. I was enjoying the music as they had an excellent violin player in the band. After dinner we went for a ride. Calendra rode in an enormous limousine with his wife, a frail old little lady. Calendra said: "Thommy boy", that's how they called me, "you drive the car". An invitation I eagerly accepted as I had always wanted to drive one of those big American cars. We were followed by four other cars. "You drive very well," Calendra said to me. After some time he said: "We're going for a stroll in the park to help digest our food." It seemed a strange surrounding to me and I felt uneasy, although I couldn't explain why.

So we were strolling in the park with Calendra and his wife, both of them dressed in their finest. We were just chatting a bit about the Netherlands and muay thai. I sat down on one of the benches with Calendra and his wife and chatted a bit more. I saw Verstraeten and Finot sitting on a bench together and wondered by myself: Why are they sitting over there with just the two of them? After a while it was decided we would return to the hotel. At that point I saw Verstraeten turning as white as a sheet of paper, I mean he looked paler than a ghost. It surprised me as he seemed to be quite the gentleman. Finot was laughing all the time. When we got back at the hotel Verstraeten poured it all out. They had said to him: "Verstraeten, you shouldn't play around with Thom Harinck like that. As a punishment you must pay for your own ticket and you're not allowed to come to the US again. And if you continue like that you won't leave the park alive." This is of course not my world, but I did experience it. The song they played live in the restaurant at our table that I enjoyed so much was actually a death march that conveyed you were eating your last supper.

The next day Verstraeten boarded a plane back to France with a ticket he paid for himself. He never again played a role in the French muay thai organization and I later learned that he had ripped off the organization. The next day I taught my seminar. The gym was enormous and modern. The entire hall was filled with Italian studs with great physiques, but they hadn't the faintest idea of what muay thai was about. Loads of people had come to watch and the press was also present.

You'll understand by now that Finot was no angel, but he never lied to me and could walk the talk. Only a few days later when I was back in the Netherlands I saw on the news or read in a newspaper that a mafia boss had been arrested. It turned out to be the owner of the gym I gave my seminar at. He was later sentenced to 25 years imprisonment. Since then the clan has thinned out; all of the members have either passed away or have been murdered.

Finot was dating a Belgian woman at some point. The girl committed suicide, at least that's how the story goes. I never believed that. She had an astronomical life insurance and he was her boyfriend. He received all the money after her death. The last time I heard his voice was in 1995. He phoned me and said: "Thom, I'm coming to see you in two weeks time." During that period I had several contacts in Belgium, gym owner André Rigiani among them, who were trying very hard to catch up with their muay thai neighbors in the land of windmills.

Rigiani phoned me one day in February 1996 and said: "Finot is dead". It turned out they found his body in a well. He was of course murdered. French mobsters were responsible for his death. He was dating one of their women, which is a big no-no in the underworld. He died young; he was only in his early forties. So through my involvement in the sport I've had many pleasant and funny experiences, but also some unpleasant and crazy experiences. Fighting is a microcosm of life itself and like the age-old yin and yang symbol we all have to navigate between the good and the bad in our lives.

SPORTS CLUB OYAMA

In 1973 Jan Stapper, together with his boss Maurits de Vries whose nickname was *Zwarte Jopie* or Black Jopie (as mentioned earlier), set up a small gym that used the loft above the *Casa Rosso* as a training space. Some of the broadest shoulders in town would have to squeeze through one of Amsterdam's narrowest alleys, Kreupelsteeg, to get to the entrance of the gym. It was called Sports Club Oyama (after kyokushinkai founder Mas Oyama), commonly just known as "The Loft". Jan Stapper acted as a boss and taught kyokushinkai karate, while Willem Ruska taught judo and Chris Dolman sambo [Russian wrestling]. This gave men like Stapper, Ruska and Dolman the chance to combine their work as bouncers at Jopie's various clubs with being top athletes in their respective sports. American tourists visiting the red light district would have their picture taken with twofold Olympic judo champion Ruska, who was working for minimum wage as a bouncer. The Loft would become notorious in Amsterdam. It was said that if you became a champion in the Loft, it would be akin to a world title. Guys as big as gorillas were known to stumble down the stairs after grueling workouts.

There was a bell that would ring if there was any trouble in the streets and the men working out would rush outside to take care of it. For a certain period the red light district, guarded effectively by a privately owned security force, actually became a relatively safe neighborhood. Drugs dealers plying their trade would be sent flying into one of the canals. After several years the "security force" had to step down a bit as the police wanted to regain control of the area.

After Jan Stapper retired from teaching, we founded a new gym in "The Loft" called Doharu Gym. The Do came from Dolman, the Ha from Harinck and the Ru from Ruska. All my students of the Van Hallstraat came to train in Kreupelsteeg. They didn't have to pay. When we were finished training, Black Jopie made sure that there would be a free buffet of food and drinks. He probably did this to be able to recruit security workers for his establishments. Doharu Gym lasted for about a year. The kickboxing classes were the busiest classes. The drawback was that you couldn't park your car anywhere and after some time my motivation decreased. I preferred teaching at my own gym. So I quit and the gym ended soon thereafter. Ruska opened a pub. Chris started to train at a location in Amsterdam North. So the year 1989 spelled the end of the Loft as a place for martial arts instruction. Currently the location is being used as a black room by a nature photographer.

MY SWEET REVENGE (14 OCTOBER 1990)

On 27 May 1990 Ramon "The Diamond" Dekkers defeated Cherry S. Wanich (ranked number one of the Lumpinee stadium) in the first round with a simple left jab in Amsterdam. On 31 August of the same year, Peter "The Hurricane" Smit, knocked out Changpuek Kiartsongrit in the Lumpinee stadium with a right cross in the second round. In the same summer, Ivan Hyppolite fought Jomhod "King of the Ring" Kiatadisak, champion of both the Lumpinee and Rajadamnern stadiums. This fight resulted in a win on technical knockout for Hyppolite in the third round. It seemed as if the Dutch fighters were knocking out their Thai opponents wherever they went.

On 14 October 1990 I organized a kickboxing event together with the famous Thai promoter Sanchai that was televised live in Thailand (which had to be held in the afternoon for commercial reasons). Six top Thai competitors would fight six top fighters from the Netherlands. Ernesto Hoost won by knockout in the first round from Mr. Seyoke, one of the few Thai fighters to weigh around 80 kg. The high point was the fight of Gilbert Ballantine versus Sangtiennoi "The Deadly Kisser" Sitsurapong. Sangtiennoi was considered one of the best Thai boxers active at the time. He got his name by kissing an opponent on the forehead in a clinch situation before knocking them out. Sangtiennoi was 4.5 kilos heavier than Gilbert and also considerably taller than Gilbert.

As I said before, for the Thai fighters, it's not uncommon to use the first two rounds to feel the other guy out and keep their offensive in store for the last three rounds. In the first round Gilbert took the initiative and he ended the round with an advantage as far as points were concerned. The second round repeated the pattern established in the first round, with Sangtiennoi engaging Gilbert in the clinch to prevent him from scoring points. In the third round, the Thai started his offensive with some excellent boxing to the cheers of the Thai supporters. He had to take a couple of incredibly hard punches that would have had most folks in dreamland, but this Thai fighter seemed to have been born with a KO-proof head. In the last round Sangtiennoi began another offensive, but Gilbert was too smart and experienced to let him take control of the match. After a conspicuously lengthy deliberation on the part of the jury,

Gilbert was declared winner and world champion. Even the Thai supporters agreed with the final verdict and in the dressing room I had to wipe away a tear. What a long way we had come since that day in 1976 when all my fighters lost against top Thai opponents in a hellishly hot stadium in Bangkok!

CIKATIĆ VS ALEXIO (16 MARCH 1992, NEVADA, USA)

In 1992 Branko received an invitation to fight Dennis "The Menace" Alexio in Las Vegas for the heavyweight title of the WMAC (World Martial Arts Challenge). This was a match with low-kicks but without clinching and was to be televised on national television. Dennis Alexio was the superstar of American kickboxing around that time. Three years earlier he had starred in the movie *Kickboxer* alongside Jean-Claude van Damme. He won a lot of KOs against subpar opponents. We accepted the match. It was the same story as with the fight against Don Wilson. The Americans set up an enormous publicity campaign. Again, it was the guy from the Eastern Bloc against the American.

Come 16 March 1992 we were ready to go. When Alexio came up to the ring, he had a string of guys walking behind him carrying all of his championship belts. He had titles from all the major kickboxing organizations: PKA, IKF, ISKA, KICK and WKA. Of the two fighters, only Alexio was wearing safe-T-kicks. During the fight, Alexio handled himself well with his boxing skills while Branko scored a lot with low-kicks. A knee delivered from a clinch situation resulted in minus points for Branko. Branko also had a cut above his right eye from an illegal elbow from Alexio.

In round three Alexio tried to kick Branko in the head, but his safe-T-kick slipped off his foot. The referee saw this and called out: "Stop". So Branko turned around to retrieve the safe-T-kick. While he was standing with his back toward his opponent, Alexio delivered a double left hook to the back of the head and tried to kick him but missed. Branko went down, not understanding what had happened. The spectators were totally confused and were booing like hell. Everyone jumped into the ring, including me. The match, that was supposed to go for eight three-minute rounds, was then declared a technical draw.

When we went back to the dressing room Branko was angry as hell. He was swearing and said: "I won't stand for this". He was still wearing his gloves. We passed Alexio's dressing room. Alexio was there with about seven other guys, celebrating with the whole team. Branko charged into the dressing room and shouted: "You want to fight? Well, you can get a real fight from me! You bastard, why don't you fight fair?" And I said: "Branko, stop, you're still wearing your gloves." If you fight for real then gloves would only be a disadvantage. So I got his gloves off and then the security guys walked in. Alexio was staring sheepishly in front of him. I finally managed to pull Branko out of the dressing room and we went to our own. So with two major fights in the US I encountered similar unsportsmanlike incidents and it disappointed me. It wasn't something I expected. I mean, as far as organizing and publicizing an event is concerned, you can surely leave it to the Americans. But as far as sticking to the rules is concerned, I found them to be somewhat unfair.

Of the two fighters, Alexio and Wilson, Wilson was definitely the one whose fighting style I liked best. Alexio was more of a brawler while Wilson, with a background in white dragon (pai lum) kung fu, and was much more of an athletic fighter. Wilson actually fought Alexio once in 1984 and won on points. Alexio continued to fight up until 1999, although he seemed to avoid any big names after his fight against Branko. Don Wilson starred in a string of Bruce Lee imitation movies throughout the 1990s. He still makes occasional appearances in movies and television series when he's not producing them.

AN INTERLUDE

KIDS AND KICKBOXING

Recently there was a Dutch kickboxing coach who said on TV: "Let the children train under me because we win all our matches by knockout." This is a very stupid thing to say. They even interviewed some of the kids' parents and they said, "It will make them tough", which is equally absurd. Children should be protected. Up to the age of 12 I don't even want them to get hit in the head. From 12 years onward hitting to the head would be OK. When they're sparring I want to see gloves, head protectors and even then they should take it easy. If a child gets in a hazardous position in competition, the referee should stop the match and declare a winner. From 16 years onwards they can fight under grown ups' rules. A good coach always has the obligation to throw the towel in the ring [which signifies the end of the match] if a pupil gets too many punches or kicks. There's a doctor at ringside who can end the match at any point if he feels that the health of the participants is in serious danger. And then there's the referee who can end the match at any point he thinks necessary. If three adults say: "Stop this, this kid is taking way too many punches," they should stop the match. I totally condemn children getting unnecessary punishment in a ring. Since their brains are still developing, a knockout should not occur under any circumstances.

DISCRIMINATION

I've encountered very little discrimination in the gym in all my years of teaching. I think that there is way less discrimination in the gym than in society as a whole. If you look at some soccer matches, the supporters make ape-like noises to a team with black players, and players call the players of the other team by all kinds of names. This almost never happens at kickboxing events or in kickboxing gyms. It might have to do with the fact that in the gym, more students from minority groups train than Dutch students. It's a sort of society in reverse. I have a picture from a group I trained in the 1980s and all of them are from minority groups. In some instances a boy from a minority group might say something derogatory about a Dutch boy. Then I would say: "We don't do that in this gym, otherwise you'll have to deal with me."

DOPING

I am dead against doping. I think it's terrible. At this point I think many kickboxers in the heavyweight category use extracurricular supplements, so to say. Fighters that weighed 90 kg at one point all suddenly become 110 to 120 kg. That's just unnatural. So I am against it, but it's not checked thoroughly by most organizations. I was in Zagreb for an event in the K-1 in 2013 and they said beforehand there would be a doping check. Turned out there wasn't any at all. And in Japan the fighters have to urinate in a little pot, but some guys have a mate pee for them and they switch their urine; the control is that weak. Also it isn't exactly known what they do and don't test for. I have the feeling that even Keith Richards could test negative for these tests! We should make an example of how the UFC (Ultimate Fighting Championship (an organization for Mixed Martial Arts competition) handles this in the US. The

Nevada State Athletic Commission, an external agency, gets paid to check the fighters aren't doping.

It must have happened at my gym but never with my consent. You also see fighters getting more aggressive. There were instances when I said to a boy who was virtually gaining muscle mass overnight: "You're getting heavy. Are you using anything?" And it would be: "No, sensei, I'm not using anything." That was where it would end. I've had a fighter from Romania who was as strong as a bear, but after 2 to 3 rounds of sparring he'd be beaten. The doping doesn't improve your endurance. Although there seems to be new stuff out there that does improve your endurance. Using doping is unfair. In a fight between someone who uses and someone who doesn't, the advantage is with the user. The punches and kicks have more impact, the user will be physically stronger. Just like they're trying to clean it up in cycling, I think we should do the same in kickboxing. There was a time when I was looking into natural remedies like acupuncture as an alternative. We were out in nature a lot, so I tried to make healing salves. But I never really became an expert in this field.

CHAMPIONS IN THE 1990S

CORRINE GEERIS

Corrine Geeris was my best female pupil. She won a K-1 tournament that I organised in 1995 with Johan Vos. This was the first tournament ever held for women. She fought against an Australian woman, a Belgian woman and an English woman. Later in her career Corrine fought a couple of boxing matches, at some point the boxing organisation had her choose between Thai boxing and boxing, the boxing league is that short-sighted in the Netherlands. In most other countries this would never be a problem.

There are a lot of tournaments for women in Japan, both in kickboxing and MMA. The girls are like dolls, with an average weight of 50 kg. As far as spectators are concerned it's a 50-50 division between men and women.

PATRIK "THE FIGHTING VIKING" ERIKSSON

Patrik Eriksson came to me when he was already a seasoned fighter. He had already trained extensively in Thailand. He slept for two years in my gym and got some extra income by re-stocking the shelves in a local supermarket. He was a very loyal Chakuriki-fighter and stayed with me until the end of his career.

Patrik once fought in Thailand against the Thai champ Coban, who was 4 kilos heavier than Patrik. He had only been training under me for a few months. Usually the Thai fighters are at the agreed weight. Patrik said: "Sen, let's do it anyway", but was knocked out after 30 seconds. In retrospect it was my mistake, I should have called it off. But professional fighters always want to fight or they'll miss their prize money.

Patrik became world champion in Johannesburg, South Africa against Makabela. The rules were kickboxing with low-kicks, no knees or elbows. South African K-1 fighter Mike Bernardo set us up against a local kid that had already several impressive wins under his belt. It was a fight over 12 rounds of 2 minutes. All of the opponents were gassed after 5 to 6 minutes of fighting. The fact is that Johannesburg is 1753 metres above sea level and if you're not used to it, going shopping is already a cardio workout. So the local guys were always eager to have people fight them on their own turf. I was there two weeks beforehand and started the first training with Patrik on the kicking pads. After just 1 minute he was gasping for air like a fish out of water. This was not at all what I was accustomed to with Patrik Erikson. Mike Bernardo was there as well and explained to me that only athletes who are accustomed to the thin air can train fully for extended periods of time. I immediately switched to a totally different game plan. I said: "Pat, don't do anything but defend. The only offense you'll use will be the low-kick".

Mike Bernardo helped us out as a corner man. It was just me and Patrik in South-Africa, so we could use an extra hand. Years earlier I had helped Mike Bernardo master the low-kick, as he was a fighter with a background in professional boxing who later sought fame in the K-1 circuit. So Mike Bernardo was returning a favour. Patrik had one of the hardest low-kicks in the business. In the first round Patrik's opponent was way more active. But Patrik slammed in his low-kick at every chance he got. He scored with five or six low-kicks every round. After five rounds the South-African could hardly stand on his legs, while Patrik hadn't used up all of his air. I let him quicken the pace in every last half minute by shouting "Chico". In the sixth round he KO'd his opponent with low-kicks. The South African couldn't stand on his legs anymore. He simply had to give up and Patrik won the world title. Not many people expected the blonde Swede to triumph in predominantly black Johannesburg, but Patrik delivered a world-class fight and was rewarded accordingly.

Later he began a relationship with a Dutch lady. He is now married with two children. I am still in touch with Patrik and he comes around to my house when he can. He is now earning a living as a successful businessman.

THE EVOLUTION OF MARTIAL ARTS

PANKRATION IN *PARADISO* (17 MAY 1981)

Chris Dolman wanted to organise an event with no-holds barred fighting that mirrored the ancient Pankration of Ancient Greece. It was held in Amsterdam's pop temple *Paradiso*. Chris organised it together with a journalist whose name was Ton van Dijk. Chris asked me if I had some participants, and of course I had. I came with four guys and one girl. The girl was Saskia van Rijswijk. She didn't have to fight, because her opponent didn't show up. The guys included Coban and Muzaffer Yamali. All my boys won their matches by way of knockout. There were wrestlers, participants from a kyokushinkai gym and an individual entry who totally got his butt kicked. The event was very crowded and Paradiso was completely full, but there were still between 300 and 400 people standing outside and they had to be sent home. This crowd of people were milling around in front of the building and even preventing the trams from passing.

Me and Chris Dolman refereed the matches. They also did some strong man stuff like tearing up telephone books. The fighting matches were a bit like MMA nowadays but in a very raw form. Head butts and biting were prohibited. Knees and elbows were our best weapons. They didn't fight on time, there was no time limit. You fought until there was a winner. Most of the fights ended very quickly though. There were no skirmishes in the hall fortunately, and all the fights took place in the ring. Later there were problems with the police who were not amused. This was the first and only event of its kind ever to be held in Paradiso.

THE FIRST MIXED FIGHT (20 NOVEMBER 1988)

On 20 October 1988 the first "mixed fight" was held in the Netherlands in which a wrestler would fight a kickboxer. The fight was between Chris Dolman's student Freek Hamaker and my student Charly Lieveld during a kickboxing event in the Jaap Edenhal. Lieveld was 20 kilos lighter than his opponent. It was a very hard match. Lieveld was more of a show-man, a great physique, good looks and a hit with the ladies. He wasn't really a star as far as kickboxing was concerned, but he had a happy-go-lucky attitude and a fighter's heart.

The fight started out relatively calmly with both fighters exploring their options. At one point Freek Hamaker jumped onto Charly Lieveld and made a choke from which Lieveld barely escaped. Lieveld tried to fight back with low-kicks but was grabbed by Hamaker when he attempted this. In the second round it was decided that elbows were allowed and Hamaker, who later said he hadn't been told about this rule, had to take a couple. Then Hamaker grabbed Lieveld in a clinch situation, threw him to the ground and applied a head lock that spelled the end of the confrontation. So it was 1-0 for the wrestlers. There was a lot of talk about a second confrontation between the two fighters, but it never came to be. Hamaker would later fight in the second edition of the UFC in 1994, while Lieveld had one more fight with a wrestler called Willie Peeters that resulted in a draw.

THE FIRST FREE-FIGHT EVENT IN THE NETHERLANDS (19 FEBRUARY 1995)

Starting in the early 1990s, a group of Dutch fighters successfully competed in *RINGS* competitions in Japan. *RINGS* was a Japanese MMA organisation especially active from 1995 to 2002. In 1995, Chris Dolman and Milco Lambrecht thought it was time to let the Dutch public get acquainted with this form of combat. The first event was held on 19 February in Sporthallen Zuid (Sport Halls South) in Amsterdam. Fighters like Dick Vrij, Hans Nijman and Herman Renting all faced Japanese opponents. Chris Dolman would fight his very last match at the venerable age of fifty against Akira Maeda; a match he won by submission in a leglock in the second round. The rules were the same as the ones used by *RINGS* Japan: all judo and wrestling techniques permitted, all kicks permitted, punching to the body and blows with the palm of the hand to the head were permitted. I participated with one student, Piet Bernzen, originally from Germany. He fought about 20 matches and won almost all of them. Piet was matched against Ronny Rivano, multiple Dutch and European karate champion who was slowly branching out into the full-contact arena. Another fighter from my gym that would later fight free-fight matches was Michael Tielrooy.

Pictures of the face of Ruud Ewoldt - whose face was so swollen after his fight against Japan's Yamamoto that his mother could hardly recognize him - were on the front pages of the newspapers. After this event I was asked to take part in a radio talk show. Erica Terpstra, Minister of Sports at the time, was furious and initiated a commission to see if the sport could be banned. She spoke about "that cage fighting". I said: "Madam, these fights were not held in a cage, you're misinformed." Every time I said something, she interrupted me. So at one point I said to her: "Madam, if you have any decency, you should let me speak." Suddenly there was a silence. There'd been an inquiry by Maarten van Bottenburg about the possible prohibition of free-fight as a sport. The inquiry concluded that free-fight, taught and organised in a responsible way, was acceptable. *RINGS Holland* was very successful in the 1990s, with Sporthallen Zuid in Amsterdam as their base, they organised many an event that sold out.

JAPAN 1990S - PART ONE

JAPAN

The first time I was invited to Japan was in 1992. Chris Dolman and his student Dick Vrij were to take part in free-fight matches for the Japanese organization called *RINGS*. I went there with Peter Aerts who would fight Adam Watt from Australia at the same event on full muay thai rules. Peter Aerts was already world champion in kickboxing and muay thai. Adam Watt is currently serving a sentence for drug trafficking that he had become involved in with Mejiro Gym's Jan Plas, now deceased. By the early 1990s, our Aussie friends had been really catching up on the sport of muay thai. This is not much of a surprise as Thailand is a favorite vacation destination for many Australians; Sydney and Melbourne especially have large Thai communities. Watt was adept at clinching and landed a few good shots before Peter knocked him out stone cold with an elbow strike in the second round. Peter immediately made a name for himself with this victory in the land of the Rising Sun.

In 1993, Kancho Ishii invited us to the first K-1 tournament. Kancho Ishii is a former kyokushinkai karate practitioner who founded his own style and organization *Seidokan* in 1980. He started toying around with different competition formats. Fights were held in a ring instead of on a mat with kyokushinkai rules: no gloves and no blows to the head. If there was no clear winner after three rounds, the fighters would put on gloves and fight two more rounds on kickboxing rules. After years of experimenting, Ishii came up with the K-1 concept: fights are held in a ring over three, three-minute rounds. But it is a tournament, which means that the winner will fight several matches during the same event to win the title. The concept is basically a marriage of the kyokushinkai tournament form, where a fighter fights numerous full-contact matches to become the champ with muay thai ring rules (minus the injury-prone elbows and the clinching that may subtract from the continuity of the match). Just like the Japanese did with Western technology, this illustrates a knack for taking things from elsewhere, giving it a twist of their own, and then marketing it with worldwide success.

Kickboxing is a generic term and unlike sports such as soccer or basketball, doesn't keep to one international set of rules. Up to the late 1980s there were three international bodies for kickboxing: the WMTA (World Muay Thai Association) for muay thai, the WKA (World Kickboxing Association) for kickboxing without knees and elbows, but with low-kicks, and the ISKA (International Sports karate Association) for American full-contact. At least for insiders, this situation was clear. But in the early 1990s, all world bodies for kickboxing started adding other competition formats to their repertoire, all with their own respective weight categories. This resulted in a multitude of champions and to the outside world the situation was incredibly confusing: it seemed as if the sport had as many champions as practitioners. Halfway through the 1990s Kancho Ishii seemed to have transformed the confusion into clarity. With the K-1 there was one organization, one set of rules, one weight category and one champion. And the champion got all the money and media attention.

Seven fighters were already lined up for the first K-1 event: Todd Hays (USA), Maurice Smith (USA), Changpuek Kiartsongrit (Thailand), Atokawa Toshiyuki (Japan), Masaaki Satake (Japan), Ernesto Hoost (The Netherlands) and Peter Aerts (The Netherlands). Ishii called me and said: "I have a place left for one guy. Do you have a heavyweight?" And I replied: "You bet I've got one. His name is Branko Cikatić". Branko was 38 years old by then and most ring fighters of that age are making their way into retirement. I said to Branko: "You can fight in a tournament and the first prize is 100,000 dollars." He immediately agreed. Branko had fought in the Netherlands, Sweden, Germany and England. The fees he got for those matches were peanuts in comparison with the prize money they offered him in Japan.

When we arrived in Japan, Branko seemed to be in the shape of his life. He faced Kiartsongrit Changpuek in the quarter finals. Changpuek, who barely weighed 80 kg, was considered a heavyweight for Thai standards but he was the lightest fighter in the tournament. The K-1 initially was an open weight category, meaning that fighters of any weight could participate. Changpuek had fought and defeated the best kickboxers in the West, including Rob "Mr. Low-kick" Kaman from the Netherlands and Rick "The Jet" Roufus from the US. With barely 30 seconds to go in the first round, Branko ended Changpuek's K-1 aspirations with a perfectly timed left hook. In the semi-finals, Branko was matched against Satake, a pupil of Kancho Ishii himself and Japan's best bet for the title. In the third round Satake found himself on the canvas after receiving a left hook from Branko he never saw coming. In the final, Branko was matched against Ernesto Hoost, who had just barely won on points against Peter Aerts. In the first round, Branko was dealt some pretty heavy blows by Hoost that didn't seem to affect him. Towards the end of the first round Branko initiated with a left lead and followed with a right hook that proved to be a one-way ticket to the canvas for Hoost. Me and all the corner men jumped into the ring - we were happy beyond belief.

So Branko became the first K-1 champion at the age of 38. Nobody had expected that a stand-in fighter of that age would win the tournament. Branko's charisma and his fighting prowess made him an instant star in Japan. We had a wonderful time in Japan and Branko would continue to fight there for several years.

THE LOST PRIZE MONEY

Branko won his first big prize money in the K-1 in 1993: 100,000 dollars. He received the money in cash in the ring when he won the tournament. Loads and loads of pictures were taken of it. He carried the cash with him back home. We always flew to Amsterdam first, and Branko would fly to Zagreb from there. I kept the money with me until we went back. He had stored the money in a money belt. The K-1 always lets the coach travel first class while the fighters and corner men travel economy class. If you're the champ you can demand to travel business class, but this was Branko's first K-1 title.

I hate flying. I'm actually scared to death of it, so I usually take a sleeping pill and just sleep through it. At some point during the flight, Branko woke me up. He was in a state and said: "Thom, Thom, I lost my money." I was wide awake immediately. Now what happened was this. Branko had taken a sleeping pill too but had gone to the toilet to answer a call of nature and had left the bag of money in the toilet. When he later realized he wasn't carrying the bag, it was no longer in the toilet.

I approached the stewardess and said: "This guy has just lost 100,000 dollars. We have to retrieve the money." Branko had brought seven guys with him from Croatia, and Branko, a full-fledged heavyweight, was actually the smallest of the group. One of them was 2.10 metres tall. These were all very big and rich guys who also had sponsored him. The stewardess wanted to say something though the microphone, but I took the microphone out of her hand and said: "We are very sorry, ladies and gentlemen, but my fighter has just lost 100,000 dollars and we will be searching everyone on the plane. We'll be starting in the front and will work our way to the back." So we started out in the front of the airplane while it was still flying, in the economy class, and politely asked people to empty their pockets and open their bags for us. About three seconds later, someone came running up from the back of the plane and said: "I think I have a bag here with something in it." So that's how Branko got his money back. To think of it, that he had almost lost 100,000 dollars! I really doubt that if the plane hadn't been searched by a bunch of large, tough gorillas, he would have ever seen that money again.

K-1 GRAND PRIX 1994

In the quarter finals Peter Aerts had to fight Rob van Esdonk. This was an interesting match in the sense that two Dutch fighters were matched against each other, both from the south of the Netherlands. Peter had already defeated Rob van Esdonk in a match six months earlier. And I stood for the umpteenth time, eye to eye with Jan Plas who was coaching Rob van Esdonk. It turned out that the reach was in Rob van Esdonk's favour. In the first round the fighters seemed well-matched. Van Esdonk even scored a knock-down, although it was partly Peter slipping on the canvas. Van Esdonk couldn't finish the job and the bell soon rang.

The second round saw Peter dominating. Rob was taking many punches but remained dangerous and Peter could smell his victory. Rob was breathing heavily and staggering, but managed to make it to the end of the round. In the third round Peter went for the kill. While Rob was busy defending against a flurry of punches, Peter launched his trademark high kick, which took Rob completely by surprise. Rob crashed to the ground like a felled tree and was still lying on the canvas after the referee's count of eight.

In the semi-finals, Peter fought former UFC-fighter Patrik Smith. Patrik started out attacking wildly. Towards the end of the first round, Peter shot out his right cross which resulted in a heavy knockout for our American friend. In the finals, a born-again Peter

Aerts faced crowd-pleaser Masaaki Satake. Satake continued to attack, but not for a moment was Peter in any kind of danger. After three rounds, Peter was proclaimed the winner by a unanimous jury decision. So Peter won his first K-1 championship at the age of 23.

K-1 GRAND PRIX 1995

In the quarterfinals, Peter was matched against Atokawa from Japan. Atokawa came up to the ring with a headband with the Japanese flag on it. Peter Aerts totally annihilated Japan's K-1 aspirations with an uppercut in the first round. He could go on to the semi-finals without having had to break into a sweat.

In the semi-finals Peter was matched against Ernesto Hoost. Hoost was coached by Johan Vos and Jan Plas, so this was a reunion of sort of the three kickboxing pioneers from Amsterdam. There was no friendliness in the ring, however. In the first round Peter dominated his opponent and Hoost was punched and kicked through the ring, but with some good hits from Hoost at the end of the round. The second round looked like a replay of the first, with Hoost scoring with a well-timed high kick. Hoost had a cut above his eye, but it wasn't serious enough to stop the fight. In the third round, both fighters seemed to be evenly matched.

After three rounds the judges scored Peter as winner of the first round, Hoost as winner of the second and the third round as a draw. This meant there would be one more round. In the last round, Peter dominated with Hoost trying to clinch a lot in order to avoid Peter's punches and kicks. Peter won the fourth round unanimously and prevented Ernesto Hoost from becoming the K-1 champ, at least for that year.

In the final match Aerts had to face Jérôme Le Banner who had already KO'd both of his prior opponents. But with approximately one minute to go in the first round, Peter connected with a body shot that left Le Banner on the canvas with a painful look on his face. This meant that Peter became K-1 champ for the second time. There was a third time to follow and Peter took part in all K-1 Grand Prix up to the year 2009.

PERRY UBEDA WINS THE ALL JAPAN OPEN ITF TAEKWONDO CHAMPIONSHIP (1996)

During the period that I was very popular in Japan I got an invitation to participate in an open taekwondo tournament with one fighter. We were put up in a luxurious hotel and could earn prize money if we placed first. I thought Perry Ubeda would be the man for the job. All of the participants wore white gis, and they were skilled technical fighters with incredible kicking techniques. There were a few Russian participants and some people from other countries as well. Most of the participants were Japanese. Perry Ubeda weighed 74 kg at the time and I enrolled him in the heaviest weight division: 85 kg- plus. The organizers first said: "That's not possible." I asked them: "Why not?" "It's in your disadvantage, we have a couple of very good fighters," they said. "We'll take that risk," I answered. Eventually they put him with the 85-plus boys.

The tournament was held in the Yoyoki stadium in Tokyo. It's a different kind of venue than the Tokyo Dome, which was originally a baseball stadium. Yoyoki has a bit more élan. There were lightweights, middleweights and heavyweights. We had to line up in rows. All of the participants were wearing white uniforms and black belts, except for Perry who was standing there in his red Chakuriki kickboxing shorts. The organizers threw a fit and said: "That's not allowed. He's required to fight in a proper uniform." Then I said: "Then he won't fight. He's a Chakuriki fighter and he'll fight in Chakuriki shorts." Eventually they gave in. So in the line with the heavyweights there were about 20 big guys and Perry in his red shorts. The whole event was televised. The Japanese have great respect for high and spectacular kicks and every time a fighter threw one there would be a loud "ooh" from the crowd, just like in the K-1.

Perry won the first round by knockout and the second round by knockout. This landed him in the final where he had to fight an excellent Japanese fighter of 108 kg. It was the final match of the evening. After three rounds, the judges said it was a draw. He had already shown that he was the superior fighter, but judges often favor their countrymen. An extra round was called for. Perry knocked him out with a reverse roundhouse kick to the jaw. He could do all of that stuff – I've seldom had such a technical fighter under my wings. It was a sight to see all of the taekwondoka's in their gis and Perry Ubeda in his shorts, with the trophy in his hands. When he stood upright on the platform he was just as tall as the guys that got second and third place. The funny thing is that Perry never took a taekwondo lesson in his life. His win was featured in magazines and the newspapers. Perry had quite thick legs, but was a natural as far as kicking and flexibility were concerned.

HELP FROM AN UNEXPECTED CORNER

While the Dutch fighters were putting a firm mark on the whole K-1 competition, the average Dutch person didn't know what the K in K-1 stood for [it stands for the martial arts that begin with a K, like karate and kickboxing]. If a Dutch tennis player should become world champion, there would be a complete welcoming ceremony at the airport led by the Minister for Sport. After winning the K-1, most Dutch champions were met at the airport just by their family and a few supporters from the gym. There seemed to be a total neglect of the sport of kickboxing within society at large.

However, help came from an unexpected corner. Mylene de La Haye is a Dutch TV-presenter and singer who is perhaps better known for her appetite for martinis and cocktails than for an affinity with martial arts and kickboxing. But in the year 2000, she presented the program *Mylene knokt door* [Mylene Battles On] on Dutch national television. Mylene was going to follow the K-1 participants from their home to the gym and to the ring. Fred

Royers provided the commentary on the matches. The program made the public aware of how significant the small country of the Netherlands is in a sport from the other side of the globe. The public also saw the fighters outside of the ring. A person might earn a living by beating up other people in a ring, but that doesn't mean they behave like that the entire day. It made people realize that professional kickboxers are just human beings like everyone else.

MY "SECRET" TRAINING METHODS

Halfway through the 1990s, some journalists from a famous Japanese martial arts magazine visited me in the Netherlands. They wanted to write an article about my training methods. We went to a sports hall with the journalists and their photographers and Branko Cikatić. I said to him: "Branko, we're going to fool around a bit here." I'm not someone who will reveal all my training systems to the first person who asks. I laid out some blocks on the floor- a training tool I normally never use in my classes. I said to Branko: "Jump!" And he had to jump from left to right and from front to back. Branko was begging me: "Sensei, please don't do this!" but I put on a very stern face and shouted: "Jump, Branko, jump." The Japanese were letting out "oohs" and "aahs" every few seconds. They were taking everything dead seriously. I put up a rope, and Branko had to jump over it. I used a wooden stick and let Branko jump over it. All things I normally never use in my classes. I let him sprint to the wall and back. At one point, that big Croatian couldn't contain himself with laughter. The Japanese copied everything verbatim and this all appeared a month later in the issue of their magazine. In the article it said something like: "that Thom Harinck sure uses some crazy training systems to get his students to championship status."

THE LAST MATCH (TOKYO, JAPAN)

Branko's last match was once more against Ernesto Hoost. During a stay in Japan, Ishii asked me into his office. I had already declared that Branko would fight one more match and that we would stop after that. He said: "I've been thinking about Branko's last fight. I want him to fight Ernesto Hoost." At that time Ernesto Hoost was *the* superstar of the K-1. He was at the height of his powers. He had won two Grand Prix and had amassed world titles in kickboxing and savate. I answered: "I understand that you want to match him against a good fighter, but to match him against Ernesto Hoost?" Ishii's answer was short and succinct: "If there's going to be a last fight, Hoost will be his opponent." Branko had already fought Hoost twice. He had won by a KO in 1993 and lost by disqualification once. So I went to the hotel room and said: "Branko, Ishii wants you to fight Ernesto Hoost in your last match, but I'm not very keen on the idea." He said: "Thom, don't worry, he can never beat me." So I said: "Fine, if you agree to this fight, we'll do it." We prepared ourselves as usual.

I've had periods when I worked fruitfully with Johan Vos, Hoost's coach, but there were also periods when there was some friction between us. As we walked over the catwalk to the ring, I saw Johan Vos standing there grinning with a face that said: "Your 40-year-old fighter is going to get his butt kicked." I'm hardly ever nervous. Well, on the inside I might be, but I don't show it on the outside. I'm a mental coach after all. But I was nervous before this fight, and Branko seemed to sense my nervousness. He put his big hands on my shoulders and said: "Thom, don't worry, he can never beat me." I wasn't being nervous without a reason, most fighters choose a walkover for their last fight, and Ernesto Hoost was no walkover.

The fight started. In the first round neither of the two fighters gained an advantage. Branko was a bit rigid as a fighter while Ernesto Hoost was very agile. I often had to shout: "Branko, move!" He tended to fight with a totally closed guard. So once again I said: "Branko, relax, move, move, move!" Branko initiated with a left lead, Hoost took Branko's left hook counter to the head and Branko countered with an accurate right cross that caught Hoost totally off guard. That cross caused an instant knockout. Hoost bounced up and down the mat several times before lying down with his limbs turned to jelly. Hoost was lying on the canvas for minutes. While in other parts of the world, one ring doctor is enough, the Japanese always have several doctors at ringside. They examined Hoost. Luckily he was alright and could take part in the prize giving in a vertical position.

After Branko received his prize, he gave an emotional speech to the public in Japan:

"I love you and I will miss you. I would like to thank Mr. Ishii. I wanted to stop fighting in 1993, but decided to continue for one more year. I will always love Japan and I would like to come back. Thank you very much, I love you. I am opening my gym in Croatia. Croatia is now going through a very difficult period. After I won the tournament last year, I couldn't train that much as I was opening my gym. Thom is my coach, my friend and my father. It's very difficult to stop. Physically and technically I still can do it all, but it's time to stop. I dedicate this match to the children of the fighters who fought for the freedom of my country. I fight for myself, for Thom, for my country and for you because you are the very best public in the world. Thank you very much!"

That was a very special moment with me and Branko both in tears. Branko got a standing ovation and some people in the crowd even had tears in their eyes. This goes to show that they were really touched as the Japanese don't normally display their emotions openly. Branko trained for 20 years under my guidance and defeating Ernesto Hoost in one's last match is the best end of a fighting career any kickboxer could wish for.

"WHO WANTS MY MONEY?"

A few months later I received a call from a Japanese free-fight organization called *Pride*. The promoter asked me if Branko wanted to fight Marc "The Smashing Machine" Kerr under free-fight rules. Marc Kerr was a wrestler from the US who fought in Japan a lot in the early 1990s. He was a good fighter, very agile and as big and strong as a bear. Kerr had been a wrestling champion at university. We agreed to the match and the prize money of 300,000 dollars, which was an exceptionally high sum in those days.

So once again we flew to the land of the Rising Sun for a fight to be held on 15 March 1998. This was a match in which ground-fighting was permitted. During the match, Branko caught hold of the ropes to prevent this. He gave his opponent several downward elbows on the head. The referee intervened and warned Branko about illegal blows. The fight continued and Branko once again took hold of the ropes. Branko was of course trying to avoid going to the ground as he had never really trained for any groundwork. Again, he caught hold of the ropes and delivered several elbows to the head. The referee handed out a red card, and that was the end of the match after barely 90 seconds. The entire hall was booing. It wasn't very smart of the Japanese. If they'd let the match continue, Kerr might have managed to get Branko to the ground, and it would've been an exciting match. This was a rare case of someone earning 300,000 dollars in a mere 90 seconds!

I had already been paid for the match. *Pride* paid me the prize money the day before the match and I had stored it in a briefcase. The briefcase was in the safe in the hotel. The next day we were drinking coffee in the hotel lobby, when suddenly seven small Japanese men in suits walked in. A few of them were carrying briefcases and all of them were missing a pinky finger. This was a clear sign that they were members of the Yakuza. The Yakuza is the Japanese version of Italy's Cosa Nostra, though the organization itself isn't outlawed in Japan. Members are obliged to cut off one of their fingers every time they screw up.

"Mr. Cikatić, Harinck-san [Harinck-san is what the Japanese always call me] we have something to discuss with you." Branko was sitting there like a prince. He'd just won 300,000 dollars in prize money and for someone from Croatia that's a fortune. The Japanese said: "Because Branko has been disqualified, we want some of our money back." So I said: "Hey Branko, they want your money back, because it wasn't a fair fight." Branko put down his cup of coffee, stood up and thundered through the lobby at the top of his voice: "Who wants my money back? Who wants my money back?" The Japanese stood there speechless for half a minute and then just said: "Thank you." They bowed several times and trotted out of the lobby like a group of penguins. The same day Branko left the country with his prize money.

Of course, it's true that he didn't stick to the rules. And if we'd been paid the next day, they might have confiscated part of the prize money and we would have been powerless. At the time in Japan it was procedure to pay fighters in cash before the fight. Nowadays it's transferred to your bank account as you're not allowed to cross the border with large sums of money.

So me and Branko went through a lot together. In daily life he is a very gentle and good-natured man, not aggressive at all. He is as benevolent outside of the ring as he is a beast between the ropes. After his retirement he set up two gyms and a security company in Croatia that had 300 employees at one point. The government had his men guard many banks and government buildings. Currently he still runs a gym. His students are not that good. He's more of a fighter than a coach. He's a bit too lazy to pass on things to others.

Branko was always very loyal towards me. We never had a written contract in all his years with me. There were many times when people tried to get him to train elsewhere. They tried to pull the same shit on me as they did with Badr Hari [see the chapter "Bad Boy" Badr Hari]: offering him a house or a car in exchange for going to train elsewhere. I later learnt that Henk de Vries, the owner of Amsterdam's first and most famous coffee shop The Bulldog [a coffee shop where soft drugs were sold], offered him large amounts of money to go and fight for Mejiro Gym. But where Badr gave in, Branko stayed loyal. For two years he slept in my gym in a small room and he would clean the gym in the weekends in lieu of rent. You don't get something for nothing in my book.

When he married, I was his best man. I went to Croatia with my wife, which was still during the war in the Balkans. We're almost family now. This year I bought a holiday home about 10 minutes' walk from his home in a small village close to Split. It's close to the sea and nice and quiet. I think me and Branko get along well because we have the same attitude to life and in fighting.

JAPAN 1990S - PART TWO

KANCHO ISHII

Ishii always drummed it into the fighters that the fees they received were secret. The fighters weren't even allowed to tell each other, as each fighter had his own fee. The funny thing is that Ishii himself later ran into problems with the tax people. When fighters were in Japan, they had to sign a document that never specified the prize money. What I suspect happened was that he declared a totally different sum to the tax service than he had actually paid the fighters. If they paid as much for a free-fight, as they paid for Branko's match against Kerr, they would pay way more for a K-1 match. I think this is also one of the reasons for the downfall of the K-1 organization.

Ishii once bought 300 Chakuriki T-shirts from me. They were sold at one of the events and there was also a T-shirt booth for Seidokan, the style Mr. Ishii had created. The Chakuriki shirts sold out within 10 minutes, while most of the Seidokan shirts were still for sale when the event was over. Ishii never really appreciated this. I was there with Peter Aerts, Branko Cikatić and a couple of lightweights as well, Gilbert Ballantine, Perry Ubeda and Patrik Eriksson among them.

Around that time I flew to Japan up to six or seven times a year. We were the most popular gym in Japan at the time. I later heard that Ishii wasn't too pleased about that. In 1999 the K-1 was at the height of its popularity with 65,000 people in the Tokyodome attending the Grand Prix. It was a beehive buzzing with people. A few times I walked out of the dome and within minutes the security had to escort me back into the hall as I was practically mobbed. I had become so famous that everyone wanted an autograph or a picture.

I made a lot of Japanese friends and started hearing things. For instance they tried to get Peter away from my gym. Ishii wanted Peter under *his* wings so he could save a lot of money. Peter once did an interview for *Playboy Magazine*, and I told him it was fine but that he should demand a few thousand dollars. I don't recall the exact fee. Peter made a lot of money from things like that. When Ishii organized the first K-1 tournament he was sleeping in his car; later he became a multi-millionaire. He transferred enormous sums of money to his Swiss bank account. All the matches were broadcast on Fuji TV and Ishii made his money through the commercials. Then there was all the merchandise. There were miniature dolls made of fighters like Peter Aerts and Ernesto Hoost, video tapes and later DVDs of all the events. I haven't even mentioned the photo rights. Ishii must have made an incredible amount of money this way. He considered me a pain in the ass, because I asked money for everything my fighters did. The money was for them of course, though I did receive a commission.

In 1997 Peter left my gym. The Japanese were telling him that I had set something up with Johan Vos concerning his contract. These were all lies and Peter later returned to my gym and fought some of the best matches of his later career under my guidance. When Peter opened his own gym it was impractical for him to travel to Amsterdam every morning. He has since found a new coach close to his hometown. He asked me to coach him during the match and do his preparation in his own gym, but I declined. I have to be present also during the preparation in order to coach a fighter effectively during the match.

MR. ISHII'S KEYS

Johan Vos, Mr. Ishii and I once got together in a pub in Japan to talk business. This was in the beginning of the K-1 and fighters got around 5,000 dollars for a match. We wanted to impress on him that this was too little and the prize money for fighters should be raised. Japanese people don't get mad very easily and Ishii was always very polite towards us trainers, since he needed us. He had been drinking a bit that evening and at some point during our discussion he became furious. He grabbed his car keys, threw them on the table with all his strength and then walked out. Me and Johan Vos looked at each other and thought: What's up with him? He didn't agree with us and he gave vent to his anger in his own way. We waited about 15 minutes for him to return, but he never came back. Ishii drove in an incredibly big, red Lamborghini. So I picked up the keys and drove back to the hotel in his car. The next day he embraced me and it was "Oesh, sensei" as if nothing ever happened. I gave him back his car keys and we never spoke about the incident again.

PETER "THE HURRICANE" SMIT

Peter Aerts left my gym in 1996. Ishii had told him that I was screwing around with his contracts. In the meantime, Peter Aerts had struck up a friendship with Peter "The Hurricane" Smit, a former European and Open Pacific champion in kyokushinkai karate. After he switched to kickboxing, he became world champion with the International Muay Thai Federation in 1990; knocking out the Thai champ Changpuek Kiartsongrit with an elbow in Bangkok's Lumpinee Stadium.

Two years after Peter Aerts left my gym, I went to Tokyo with Nobu

Hayashi. Peter was on the same plane with his new trainer and Peter Smit who came along as a supporter. By then Peter Smit had ended his fighting career due to an ankle injury. Peter Smit seized the opportunity to partake in the free drinks that were being served during the flight and was pretty boozed up after a few hours. He walked down the aisle and spat me right in my face. He accused me of stealing money from Peter Aerts. I didn't react; you can't be fighting on a plane. So I just said: "Look fellow, walk away," while I wiped his spit off my cheek. Luckily he walked on. When we arrived in Japan he was so drunk that he could hardly stand upright. He started again, and once again I didn't react. Although, in the state he was in, I could probably have knocked him out with a single blow. Kancho Ishii came to the airport to pick us up. They decided to put up the Chakuriki group, and Peter Aerts and his following in separate hotels. Somehow they had gotten wind of the tension between us and took measures to avoid any skirmishes that could get in the way of the tournament.

A few months later, back in the Netherlands, I was at a kickboxing event. Peter Smit was also there, and he tapped me on the shoulder. He looked like he had been drinking again. I thought: Holy shit, here comes trouble. He might be more assured of himself now that he was on neutral territory. He said: "Thom, I apologize for my behaviour on the plane. I should never have done that. I now know that you're the real deal and you're not a thief. We now know the truth. Ishii wanted to get Peter Aerts close to him." He flung himself around my neck and bought me a drink. In this way we resolved our conflict.

Peter Smit later kicked his habits, straightened out his life and started a family. However, he was shot to death in broad daylight on 15 August 2005 in a dispute about a Rolex watch. In the years following his death Peter Aerts had "Peter Smit R.I.P." stitched on his kickboxing shorts and used Bob Dylan's song *The Hurricane* to come up to the ring, in memory of his friend. The first time he wore the shorts with the text was on 23 September 2005 in a fight against

Mighty Mo in the K-1 Grand Prix in Osaka, Japan. He wore these shorts for a total of 23 fights.

NOBU HAYASHI

At the height of our popularity in Japan in 1995-1996, I often got requests for Japanese guys to train at my gym. This was usually for the period of one or two months. One day in 1998, I received a letter from Koichi Kawasaki, a promoter in a wrestling organization who is still active today. He knew an 18-year-old Japanese young man who wanted to train in kickboxing with me. For a Japanese man he was big and heavy; his name was Nobu Hayashi. I agreed to the training. Nobu had told us when he was arriving and had organized accommodation. He slept in a Japanese restaurant close to Amsterdam RAI. They had lodgings for people who worked there and some extra free space.

Me and my son Thommie went to the airport to fetch him. We were told to look for a big guy. A lot of Japanese left the airplane, most of them were small, and a few were overweight. We didn't appear to see our guest. Of course we were looking for someone with an athletic build. Then we saw a tall Japanese young man, about 18 years old. His hair was very long and he had made it stand upright, he was all spotty and clearly overweight. We didn't think it was our man. At some point he approached us and said in broken English: "Oesh, Oesh, Harinck-san." I said: "Nobu Hayashi?" It was our man. Thommie and I exchanged glances in amazement.

We brought him to the Japanese restaurant. The next day he took part in his first training. He couldn't do all that much, but you could see that he had some training under his belt. The problem was his love handles. The funny thing is that within the time span of one year we got him from 135 to 112 kg, and he gained much fighting skill. He learnt to box pretty well and his kicks also improved. He wasn't the most flexible guy in the gym, but his kicks surely had impact. As a person he was calm and civilized. He was from one of the smaller islands of Japan and not from a major city.

I let him fight in the N-class and he won. Then I let him fight in the C-class. He won again. At some point he decided to stay in the Netherlands but would visit Japan every couple of months for his visa and stuff like that. We managed to get him his own flat in an apartment building and everything was fine. After he had trained with us for almost two years, he fought his first A-class match against Gurhan Degirmencia, of Turkish background, who was at that time a pretty famous fighter. Nobu won by KO in the third round.

Then Mr. Ishii organized an event, the "K-1 Championship of Japan" with 16 fighters. The champion would have to fight four matches to win the title. I was there with Nobu on 22 August 1999. Absolutely nobody in Japan knew who Nobu was. His first match was against one of Mr. Ishii's Seidokan fighters, Masaaki Miyamoto. Nobu had been through a complete metamorphosis since the day we had picked him up at the airport. His hair was short and his physique was athletic, though he never became completely shredded.

He won his first match by knockout. Amazement all around. In his next match he was again paired with another of Ishii's boys, Issei Nakai. Again, he won by knockout. In his third match he had to fight Tsuyoshi Nakasako, a very tall Japanese guy nicknamed "Labrador" because of the dog kennel that he owned. Nobu won this match on points which meant that he would be fighting in the final against Musashi, the Japanese Heavyweight superstar in the K-1. Nobu lost against Musashi on points.

Shortly thereafter a crew from a Japanese martial arts magazine came over to the Netherlands for a special feature on Nobu Hayashi and his training partner Lloyd van Dams. The feature included pictures of Nobu cleaning the toilets in the gym. Nobu was invited to talk shows and had gone from a nobody to a celebrity in his own country, on the basis of a single tournament.

There was an Englishman involved in the K-1 that I sometimes spoke to. He had spoken to Ishii about the tournament and Ishii had confided in him: "I was shocked that this unknown young man did so well". A Japanese man who can fight in the open weight category of the K-1 is worth his weight in gold. The Japanese like to see their own people become champions. They are no different in this respect than any other people on the planet. The K-1 began as a platform for Mr. Ishii to showcase his seidokan students, but before long it was the Dutch fighters who were flying back home with the titles. A Japanese in league for the title, could get the whole of Japan in front of the television.

After Peter Aerts left my gym, the K-1 matched Nobu against Peter in Japan in 2001. Nobu fought an unworldly match against Peter. But what happened was this: Nobu had sparred one of Branko Cikatić's students the day before in the gym. So Nobu had taken several low-kicks and had some trouble with his legs and Peter dished out a couple of hard low-kicks - his strongest weapon. He fought five rounds against Peter, and although Nobu lost the match, this is a feat no other Japanese, with the exception of Musashi, could emulate.

Nobu got a fight against Alexey "The Red Scorpion" Ignashov from Russia, a runner-up for the title, in 2002. In the first two rounds Nobu got a terrible beating, but after that he started to fight back. The fourth round was a draw. And the fifth for Nobu. You would think this would be a draw, but they awarded the victory to Ignashov. Ignashov, however, was completely wrecked after the fight. He had gone on one of his drinking binges the night before. He was already a heavy drinker at that point. This was a fantastic match.

The K-1 organized another event with only Japanese fighters called "K-1 Beast 2004", but this time with eight fighters. Again Nobu made it to the final in which he fought Hiromi Amada. This was Amada's farewell match. Amada was a Japanese champion in amateur boxing before he switched to K-1. He was there with his wife and his two little kids. After three rounds neither fighter had an advantage, so there was an extra round. Nobu won that round, but they decided to give the match to Amada anyway. They didn't want a Chakuriki fighter as a winner. The winner of this tournament was to take part automatically in the final eight of the world. This honor went to Amada.

Nobu trained for about four and a half years at my gym. After his fight against Peter, he got to know a girl and fell in love. Their relationship lasted for two years, but then the girl decided to end the engagement. At that point I suddenly missed Nobu in the gym. He didn't attend any classes and didn't pick up the phone when I called, so I drove over to his apartment. Someone had given me the key. When I entered the apartment he was sitting in the living room, slumped over a chair with all the curtains closed. I asked him what the problem was, but didn't get a coherent answer. He seemed very depressed and I feared he might commit suicide. I said to him: "You go back to Japan, you look up Mr. Ishii, enlist in the Seidokan-style, which means you'll be favored. You'll be the best Japanese fighter and Ishii will take care of you." It seemed as if fire was coming out of his mouth. "No, I'm a Chakuriki man, I'll die a Chakuriki man."

So I sent him back to Japan and he started a Chakuriki gym over there. Nobu is the Branch Chief for Chakuriki in Japan. He started teaching and with success. He had several young boys winning championship titles, one young man won the youth K-1 title [maximum age of 16 years]. A very promising young fighter.

Suddenly we were told that Nobu had been hospitalized. He was diagnosed with leukemia, the same kind of cancer that killed K-1 Champion Andy Hug. Luckily it didn't kill Nobu after two weeks as happened with Andy, but it did keep him in the hospital for six months.

The first place I went to when I visited Japan the next time was the hospital. I went there with Thommie and a friend of Nobu's called

Amai. I went to his room. He looked very ill and had lost a lot of weight. I updated him about how things were going in the Netherlands and suddenly I saw a smile on his face. When we left the hospital, Amai said to me: "That's the first time in four months that I saw a smile on Nobu's face." I went back to the hospital several times in the four days I was in Japan. And guess what? Two months later he was healed and could be discharged from the hospital. My visiting him really meant a lot to that young man. I couldn't let him down, he was a former student of mine.

When I visited the hospital he told me that during the time he was on the brink of dying, not a single person of the K-1 organization came to visit him. No Mr. Ishii, no Tanikawa (president of the K-1 2003-2012), nobody from the board of directors. And Nobu was deeply disappointed. I really gave them hell about this at a press conference. I told all who would listen that it was a great shame that nobody visited him.

After his release from hospital he picked up teaching martial arts and fought a few matches in Japan. One year later he was back in the hospital. The same disease had returned. In that period I was in Japan once and visited him again. He was later released from hospital and is still being monitored. You can see that the disease has taken its toll. He walks all humped over and doesn't look like the athlete he used to be. But he continues to teach at Chakuriki Japan. He deserves respect because of his fighting spirit. During the first few weeks at the gym he was almost beaten to death by all my champions. Being a big guy, he had to take countless punches and kicks. But after a few weeks, he started to punch and kick back. His fighting spirit earned him a well-deserved place in the Chakuriki hierarchy.

THE YEARS 2000-2014

PANCRATION GYM

I started in 1972. My first gym was in Cliffordstraat. The next location was in Fanius Scholtenstraat, where I lived. I had a bicycle shed there that was slightly bigger than the place we had before. Then we went to Van Beuningenstraat. We had tidied up the entire building, but learned it was to be demolished. The owners had not told us. I wrote a letter to council member Verheij who belonged to the Communist Party. He sent a guy to take a look and through him I got the gym in Van Hallstraat. It was formerly used as a boarding school for children whose parents who were away on barges. It was in Van Hallstraat that the big names came, like Gilbert Ballantine, Peter Aerts and Branko Cikatić.

During the late 1990s I sold the building to my right-hand man Erwin van der Meulen, but continued to train my competition group in the gym twice a day. The students could do bag training in the mornings. I had always been the boss and Erwin was my assistant. When Erwin became the owner, people still came to me for advice. There's only one Thom Harinck, there can't be two. That caused a collision between us at some point. So I left and started a new gym in Amsterdam North in 2002. The entire competition group followed me to the new location.

I phoned Chris Dolman, because I didn't have the money to start up. I said to Chris: "This school is for sale so shall we buy it? I don't have any money. Shall we start a gym?" Chris replied: "No, there's a whole lot of work involved." When I said: "I'll do the work, I just need the money," Chris agreed. Chris and I have been close friends since we were little boys. The gym began with 40 members and two years later we had 300. We chose the name Pancration Gym, referring to the old art of Pancration, a "no-holds barred" fighting competition in ancient Greece.

I've been teaching non-stop from 1972 to 2013. In 2011 I sold my share of the gym to Chris, but still had the arrangement that I taught classes. I would train my competition group at 10 am each day. Chris was fine with this arrangement since it brought a lot of people to the gym. I had quite a few people from abroad who followed a single lesson and Chris would receive the payment. In 2012, Chris passed the ownership of the gym on to his daughter Sharon and son-in-law Ali. However, he still can be found daily in the gym where he comes to teach and train.

My son from my first marriage, Thommie, always assisted me with teaching in the gym. He is known in the world of martial arts as the best pads man on the planet [person who holds up the kicking and punching pads for a fighter]. And I'm not saying this because he is my son. He basically started out in my classes as a toddler. He fought 22 matches in the ring, winning 21 and losing only one. He was a born athlete, he could play tennis very well and excelled in soccer. He had some trouble, though, with focusing on one thing at a time. For many years he was the pads man in Team Aerts, and he and Peter Aerts got along very well.

In the beginning I would do everything myself. Teaching classes, holding up the pads, writing out training schedules. When Branko Cikatić became the first K-1 champion in 1993, I was still doing all the pads work myself. I have a friend whom I've known since I was a boy who is now a doctor and they said: "Thom, if you're doing three times 15 rounds of pad work every day, with heavyweights that carry more than 100 kg behind their kicks and punches, you've got to watch out for your physical health." So I gradually did less of this. My son is taller than I am and weighs 100 kg. So he took over the pads work from me. It was my intention to pass on the gym to him, but he was interested in other sports including motocross. I have branches in Japan and Brazil. It would have been nice to still have a branch in Amsterdam, where I would function in the background, but that was not to be.

THREATS

In 2011, my wife Marjan was asked to sit on the supervisory board of Ajax. There was a board of five people, including Edgar Davids and Paul Römer. They said: "We're looking for someone new, perhaps a lady." Marjan is an expert in sports law and knows everything about things like transfers and state subsidies, because it's her specialism. This was an honorary position, meaning you weren't paid for the work, but you could declare your expenses, which Marjan regretfully never did. They'd have meetings six times a year.

To make a long story short, Marjan didn't agree with the course of action that Johan Cruijff had decided upon [Cruijff was a club legend with considerable influence as an advisor]. Jaap de Groot, head of sports for *De Telegraaf* [a pro-Cruijff national newspaper], and Johan Cruijff had decided that Tscheu la Ling [former top soccer player] should become the boss. He could manage working two days for Ajax. So Marjan researched into all the options. If you want to be the CEO at Ajax, you should be available for seven days a week. It's not some kind of part-time job. Eventually she decided against Ling becoming CEO. She talked this through with the board and they agreed. He couldn't become CEO under these circumstances. They started looking out for someone else to become CEO.

This then became the start of a feud with Johan Cruijff. Although he was supposed to be part of the team, Cruijff could never be reached for meetings. Also, you're not allowed to speak openly in the media about a business listed on the stock market. Marjan remained silent, but Cruijff talked. This was featured one-sidedly in the newspapers. Cruijff was frustrated that he didn't get his own way, so he started sabotaging everything. Jaap de Groot set up a hate campaign in the newspapers, against Marjan and Steven ten Have [another supervisory director], who were publicly ostracized. Marjan was working almost 24 hours a day for Ajax, because the board of directors was not functioning properly. At one point leaving the supervisory board was the only option left, so she and two other members left at the same time.

Around that time, Johan Derksen, a former top soccer player turned celebrity journalist, spoke about my wife on television. He called her a "hockey bitch" and a "country singer". He said: "What would a girl from Amstelveen know about soccer?" In fact, Marjan isn't even from Amstelveen [a town close to Amsterdam known for its many hockey players]. She was raised in the north of Amsterdam by ordinary parents. She was never a member of "high society". The fact that she mingles in the top of business and academic circles is a consequence of dedication, hard work and expertise. Indirectly I managed to get the phone number of one of Derksen's close colleagues and said to him: "Please pass this message on to Derksen. You can say things about Ajax or Steven ten Have, but leave my wife out of this. I won't let her be publicly ostracized or I'll be standing on your doorstep. I would gladly serve a one-year prison sentence for giving you a good beating." Derksen never spoke publicly about my wife again.

At one stage we also got a threatening message that contained the most vile threats such as: "We know where you live and we'll drown your children." It made my blood run cold. The message was sent by e-mail. It's no big deal nowadays to get someone's e-mail address, especially someone who works as an academic, as the e-mail addresses are always published on the university's website. We had a couple of guys in the gym who knew that I was married to Marjan, but most people didn't know this as Marjan uses her maiden name for her legal and academic work. The message was signed with a number. This is common among soccer hooligans, as they use the number of their chair in the stadium as an alias. One of the guys I was training at the time knew someone who was one of the best-known Ajax fans of Amsterdam. Anyway, the next time I saw him in the gym I asked: "Could you find out for me who this guy is from section 410? This number will help identify him."

The next day I had the name and address of the man that sent the threatening message to Marjan, so I said to her I would handle it. I got into my car and drove to his home in the east of Amsterdam. I rang the bell and a few seconds later I heard heavy steps walking down the stairs, the door was opened by this incredibly big and overweight ultra hooligan with Ajax tattoos over his entire body. When he saw me he yelled out: "Hey, Thom Harinck. What's up?" I replied: "You threatened my wife." "Impossible, that can't be true," was his reply. I said: "Her name is Marjan Olfers." He turned ashen right before my eyes. I was pretty upset. I mean, I can tolerate a lot of things in life, but not my family being threatened. I grabbed him by his shirt and said: "Listen, if you ever say anything like that about my wife again, you'll regret it for the remainder of your days on this earth. I want you to write a letter of apology this very same day."

His reaction was: "Yeah, but sorry, Thom, I never knew she was your wife. You can read it in the newspapers. They're destroying Ajax and I love Ajax." I replied: "I understand that, young man. But you shouldn't believe everything that's written in the newspapers. If my wife has a quarrel with Cruijff, they can argue as adults, but you don't threaten my wife."

The very same day my wife received an e-mail in perfect Dutch that said: "I'm sorry, Mrs. Olfers. I didn't mean it that way. I will never do it again." In total I had to make three visits like this. All of these individuals were unaware that Marjan Olfers was my wife. After these three visits, we never received a single threatening message again. Luckily, three visits did the job. I mean, you won't be able to fight a stadium full of hooligans, even if you're the best fighter on the planet. I only told Marjan about the visits afterwards. She said: "You shouldn't have done that, it will be bad for my career." But I said: "I won't let anyone threaten you." That's a bit of the samurai in me. I won't bother other people, but if they bother me they can count on repercussions.

There were a few fighters in my group who got along well with Marjan who were also Ajax fans. They said: "We won't stand for this." The students will always defend their teacher. The core of supporters is subdivided into different groups. Luckily I was able to prevent a confrontation between these groups of supporters, especially because it was the last thing that Marjan wanted. If there had been some kind of clash between these two groups it would have been pretty ugly.

I was in Romania for a fight with Raul Catinas and I was taking a look at my wife's Twitter account. Someone had written: "Bitch this and bitch that." Hesdy Gerges and the other guys who knew about the whole Ajax thing, were sitting beside me. The account of the guy that posted the message was undersigned with the firm he worked for. So I googled the firm and found their telephone number. Apparently the twitter post was from an Ajax hooligan in the province of Friesland, in the north of the Netherlands. So I phoned the company and asked whether he was in. They said: "No, he's not in today, what do you want from him?" I said: "He's an old pal of mine and I want to surprise him. We went to school together. Could you give me his phone number?" I called the number they gave me and immediately got him. "Hello, this is…" [name withheld]. "This is Thom Harinck." He knew a thing or two about martial arts, as he recognized my name: "Oh yeah, Thom Harinck," he said over the phone. I said to him: "I just read what you wrote on Twitter. What's this? You wrote: We must drown her. Why did you write that?" He could do nothing but stammer. "What's your age?" I asked him. "17". Then he said: "All of them are doing it, Mr. Harinck." Which is true, as all these fans are working each other up. "You're in Friesland, Ajax is from Amsterdam," I said. "I'm a true fan," he replied. "Has my wife ever done you any wrong?" "No, but we read this and that in the newspapers." I told him: "You don't do this again. I want you to write an apology in which you take back your rude language and promise you won't ever do it again." Ten minutes later a post appeared on Twitter: "I offended Mrs. Olfers which I shouldn't have. It won't ever happen again."

I could have done this 100 times. All of the threatening messages are still in my possession, I kept them in case I ever needed them as evidence. I said to my wife: "I think it's better not to take on such a position again." Sport and emotion go hand in hand, that's just how it is. Now she's on the supervisory board of directors of a company for which she is paid properly and it causes no trouble. I'm very glad that this whole nasty affair is now behind us.

FIGHTING 24/7?

My respected colleague and kickboxing coach Lucien Carbin, who is also from Amsterdam, once said in an interview: "If I watch a soccer match, I can give it my attention for 10 to 15 minutes, after that I'm thinking about fighting." That doesn't go for me at all, though I understand what he means. It's something I can turn on and off at will. I enjoy watching a wide variety of sports, from ice skating to the Tour de France. But the greater part of my life has been dedicated to fighting, whether it's been organizational work, thinking of strategies or combinations, teaching or designing training programs. There are 24 hours in a day. I use 8 of these hours to sleep. The remaining hours of the day will be dedicated to fighting. If I want to watch a soccer match, I'll focus on the match.

But after the match is finished my thoughts will return at once to my own world."

PETER "THE LUMBERJACK" AERTS

Peter Aerts came to me in 1990. He was trained by Eddy Smulders, a boxing champion who also taught kickboxing. Peter had just become an A-class fighter, but at some point he stopped progressing. He was then advised at his old gym to come to me. The first time he came to my gym he came with his father. At first I couldn't understand him, his accent from the south of the Netherlands was so strong. Now he speaks even more unintelligibly with all the punches and kicks he's had to take to his head. I would always say: "Pete, what are you saying?" After some time, I started to understand him. He was a very rigid fighter and his form was never outstanding. He was a redneck, but in the positive sense of the word. He was a true lumberjack, and it was me who gave him his nickname. If he had to take a few punches or kicks in a fight, you'd be sure as hell he'd give them back and probably twice as hard.

I saw that he had potential. He fought a couple of matches and won them. One of his first matches under my tutelage was against Frank Lobman in Rotterdam. It turned out to be a true slug fest. Lobman turned 38 that same day, while Peter was only 18. Peter got a terrible punishment in the first two rounds. After that Lobman became tired. Peter assaulted Lobman's legs with low-kicks so that Lobman was waggling on his legs in the last round. Peter won the match clearly as he had put three of the five rounds on his name. Altogether, Peter was to fight Lobman three times. The second time he won by KO in the first round and the third one he won by KO in the third round. He made a name for himself with these hard matches.

Peter also fought Maurice Smith, a kickboxing champion from the US, in France under full-contact rules. Peter won on points. Smith said: "I'd rather fight Peter on muay thai rules, they suit me better."

I organized the event in Sporthallen Zuid. Peter almost beheaded Maurice Smith with a high kick in the second round. It seemed to take ages for Smith to get up. Maurice Smith was a really nice guy and I took him to the airport the next day. He was still somewhat dazed after his adventure in a Dutch ring the day before.

I was at a *RINGS* event in Japan in 1992 where Peter KO'd Adam Watts from Australia with an elbow. I was there with Chris Dolman, Dick Vrij, Hans Nijman and Bert Kops. This was Peter's first match in Japan and this is how he came under the attention of Mr. Ishii who invited him for the K-1 tournament the following year. It was the beginning of our participation in K-1 finals that lasted many years.

Recently, Peter fought his last match in Japan against Rico Verhoeven, the up and coming talent from the Netherlands. He lost the match on points and in my opinion shouldn't have accepted it. The older guys think they'll do OK against the young guns, but the reality is often different. As a coach I would never have gone along with that choice. I would have said: "Fight a famous guy, but someone of about your own age." That young kid will be able to say: "I defeated Peter Aerts," while he wouldn't have stood a chance if he had fought Peter when he was 20 years younger.

THE DIAMOND

Of all the champions that came from the Netherlands, the one I like the best is Ramon "The Diamond" Dekkers. He never fought Dieselnoi as they were from different periods in time. Ramon Dekkers was a Thai boxer who fought with a western style, and he was very mobile. He was a different type of fighter than Gilbert Ballantine, for example, who was even more mobile. Gilbert and Ramon fought three times. Of the three confrontations, Gilbert won two and Ramon one. Many Thai fighters have difficulty with the mobile western style of fighting. If you were standing still, you'd have your work cut out. But fighting while standing still is something Ramon Dekkers was very good at. He could fight from either a right or left stance.

Dekkers was a champion among champions, to be honest. Very few, if any, western fighters have been able to repeat his fight record. The Netherlands has produced world champions like Rob Kaman, Peter Smit, Gilbert Ballantine and Rik van de Vathorst. All of them were able to defeat the Thai fighters and win championship titles in multiple forms of kickboxing. But Ramon Dekkers is just a bit above them. He was able to consistently defeat the Thai fighters on their own turf with their own weapons. He cemented his reputation by knocking out Coban Lookchaomaesaitong in the third round on 3 September 1991 in the Lumpinee stadium. He sent Coban spinning with an elbow and finished him off with a combination of punches. This was the second match of a feud that lasted four matches in total, with both men scoring even with two wins each. After his retirement from the ring, Ramon became a trainer at the successful team *Golden Glory* in Breda. Sadly, Ramon Dekkers passed away in 2013 at the age of 43. He had a heart attack while riding his bike. My thoughts are with his friends and family.

"BAD BOY" BADR HARI

There once was a little boy called Badr Hari. He was born in Amsterdam of Moroccan parentage in 1984. At the age of seven Badr took his first kickboxing class. He himself had wanted to take horse riding lessons but the kickboxing gym was all that the family could afford. Under the guidance of former world champion Mousid Akamrane, the young Badr quickly mastered the basics and fought his first match at the age of 7. During the 1990s, Mohammed Ait Hassou was very successful with his gym, called Sitan Gym in Amsterdam. He was also head of a flowering organisation, the WPKL [World Professional Kickboxing League] that regularly organised kickboxing events in Sporthallen Zuid, including several Netherlands-Thailand match-ups. It was only logical that Badr switched to the Sitan Gym in his early teens and fought several matches for them. When Sitan Gym decided to relocate to Rotterdam, continuing his training with them became impractical for Badr. So it came about that the then 16-year-old young man enlisted at the Chakuriki Dojo in Van Hallstraat.

Badr was a difficult young man, but then many teenagers are

difficult. He didn't have a good relationship with his father who was often away. His mother was a very friendly lady, as was his sister. He also has a younger brother. I had a positive influence on him – he listened to me. Badr was a bit of a show-off, but extremely talented as far as kickboxing was concerned.

One of my best friends is a Moroccan man who works as an engineer in The Hague. He regularly advises the Moroccan embassy. Sometimes I'd have both Badr and my friend around the house and they would chat easily as they were both Moroccans. Badr didn't have much to do between workouts and I'd sometimes bring him home with me, something I didn't usually do with other students. He would occasionally dine with my family. Before the It's Showtime event in 2004 [event organised by Simon Rutz in Amsterdam Arena], the organisation published a magazine with interviews with all the fighters. Badr was to fight Aziz Khattou and stated in the interview that we had a "father-son relationship".

Badr gained notoriety in the Netherlands by being featured in the documentary *Fighter's Heart* that was broadcast on Dutch television in 2003. It featured a 17-year-old Badr Hari alongside Rachid el Haddads, another student of mine. What we see in the documentary is a foreshadowing of what would happen. We see an extremely talented kickboxer who is reluctant to put in the necessary roadwork. The film ended with Badr winning the Dutch title at an event called Victory or Hell, in Van Hogendorphal in Amsterdam.

BADR HARI VS ALEXEI IGNASHOV (8 June 2003)

In June 2003, Melvin Manhoef was unable to fight in Amsterdam Arena as he was being detained in an Eastern European country. He was scheduled to fight in Amsterdam Arena Russia's Alexey Ignashov, the rising star of the K-1. The organiser Simon Rutz asked me if I had anyone that could replace him. That wasn't usually a problem as I had plenty of top fighters and most of them were at least 90 per cent ring-ready throughout the year due to the heavy workouts. So I suggested Badr Hari. Simon Ruts agreed and so Badr got his first chance to show the world what he was made off. Although Ignashov had beaten Sem Schilt by a knockout in the first round at the event the year before and weighed 20 kg more than Badr, young Badr didn't seem to be intimidated at all during the first round. Both fighters were trying each other out and Badr even scored several points. In the second round, Badr scored with a spinning kick that seemed to wake Ignashov up from his slumber. In the third round playtime was over. Badr scored with a clear cut cross and swept Ignashov to the ground. Half a minute later, Ignashov ended the match with a body shot to Badr's liver. Ignashov helped Badr to his feet. Badr shed a few tears while the crowd gave him an ovation. That night the sport of kickboxing had a new star.

BADR TURNS BAD BOY

I sometimes had people on my doorstep who were looking for Badr when he'd been up to mischief. Those were unpleasant moments, but I protected him because he always behaved correctly towards me. He was super polite, it was always: "Yes, sensei. No, sensei". He was very polite towards my wife as well. He would train hard in the gym. Sometimes there were problems at school and I'd be angry and tell him off. There would be certain individuals who would come and watch a class, which is fine by me, but then they'd be there every day and I'd have to send them away. They'd come in a big car, their pockets bulging with money, wearing the most expensive watches etc. They would sit at the bar and Badr would leave with them. At one point I said to them: "Don't come to my gym, Badr has to train here. If you want to make appointments, do so outside of the gym." I didn't want that kind of people in my gym. They obeyed me, but then Badr would see them elsewhere. He was clearly getting in with the wrong crowd.

The better a fighter he became, and more well-known, the more hangers-on he attracted. In December 2009, Badr told me: "I'm going on vacation to Brazil." I said: "Have a great time!" He even said his farewells. A few weeks later it turned out he wasn't in Brazil at all. On the day of my birthday, 22 December, he didn't call me. In previous years he'd always give me a ring to congratulate me. A few days later I was browsing the martial arts forums on the web and I read that Badr had signed with Simon Rutz. It turned out he had left my gym to train elsewhere.

When asked about the reason for his departure, Badr said: "Thom Harinck steals money from his fighters", which is bullshit. I have never stolen from my boys. The 20 percent I receive is normal for a trainer. Badr had hardly made any money by that point in his career. I got really mad at Simon Rutz at one stage and drove down to his office. He wanted to compensate me by paying me 10,000 euros. "You can stuff those 10,000 euros up your ass!" I told him. There was tension between me and Simon Rutz for several years. Luckily, we were able to resolve our differences and I was able to participate in his events again. I have a great respect for Simon as a promoter. His events in Amsterdam Arena ranked among the best ever held in Europe.

The whole affair devastated me at the time. That young man had been a guest in my house. There were never problems or disagreements between the two of us. I put loads of time and effort into Badr's career and was promoting him as a fighter. In soccer, if a team loses several times in a row they often blame it on the coach. But Badr's losses while he was under my wings can be counted on a single hand. And then from one day to the other he just left without saying anything. If he'd just come and talked to me and said: "I'm going to train elsewhere. It will be better for my career", I would have felt bad, but accepted it. But he said nothing and just disappeared. That hurt me deeply, that's betraying me as a trainer and as a person.

Then it was Simon Rutz heralding Badr as "the best ever" in kickboxing. Badr never won the K-1. The only title he ever won with the K-1 was a 100 kg max title against a sub-par opponent called Yusuke Fujimoto. Branko Cikatić, Andy Hug, Peter Aerts, Ernesto Hoost, Sem Schilt and Remy Bonjasky are the true stars of the K-1. If Badr had taken his sport seriously, and he had the potential, he could have won the title. But he decided to go his own way.

BADR HARI VS STEFAN LEKO

Badr's first fight with his new trainers was against Stefan "Blitz" Leko, an experienced fighter in the K-1. The whole thing is a great example of how to screw things up in a kickboxing match. Badr did his preparation in three different gyms. He trained in Amsterdam with his old trainer Mousid Akamrane [a former world champion and pupil of Johan Vos], with Edwin van Os in Alkmaar, while also doing his weight training at a body-building club called The Barbarians in Amsterdam. This is a clear example of too many cooks in the kitchen. I have no problem with a fighter taking some lessons at another gym to train in a certain area that may not be my area of expertise. And while Mousid Akamrane and Edwin van Os are great coaches in their own right, listening to contradictory advice from two different experts will only lead a fighter away from victory. And then preparing for a kickboxing match with bodybuilding-style workouts is comparable to preparing for the 100-metre sprint by running marathons. Bodybuilders want to look great on stage in their Speedos. This a completely different goal from a fighter who wants more leverage in his punches and kicks. To think that Badr weighed even less during his fight against Leko than during his preceding fight; I asked myself what on earth his coach at the bodybuilding gym had got him to do. In the media Badr was shouting things like: "The match will be a piece of cake", and "Stefan Leko's going to get his ass kicked", which is a sure-fire way to get your opponent on-guard.

When Badr Hari was announced it was probably the longest walk to the ring in the history of the sport. Badr walked into the public and danced around for several minutes, giving high fives to spectators. This is a clear example of overdoing it. I understand that Badr is a showman, but if he wants to dance all night he should go to a night club. Stefan Leko, world champion with several organisations, was backed in his corner by a team of Breda's Golden Glory gym, including Ramon Dekkers and Cor Hemmers. After Leko's entrance to the ring, we all thought the fight could commence, but Badr had to do another round of dancing in the public. By the time Badr finally came into the ring, Stefan Leko was virtually emitting sparks. During the stare-down the referee could hardy keep the two men apart.

When the fight began Badr seemed very tense. He came charging in like a blind man and as a result most of his techniques missed their target. After just 1 minute and 15 seconds, Leko placed a spinning side kick right in Badr's liver. Badr was still lying cramped with pain on the canvas after the referee's eighth count. So it turned out that Leko was the one to win in the first round by knockout. There was sheer exuberance in the Golden Glory camp. Now it was Stefan Leko and his Golden Glory mates who were dancing, but this time in the ring. It took minutes before Badr had recovered sufficiently to even stand up. When he wanted to say a few words in the microphone he was booed away by the crowd. He would later say that he had never experienced such ungratefulness. But that's what's going to happen if you're boasting before the match and lose in such a way. Badr was brutally knocked out in a match-up that potentially could have had him as a winner. I don't think Badr was too young for a fighter of Leko's level. If you think of Mike Tyson, he was only 20 when he became world boxing champion for the first time.

Badr got another shot at Stefan Leko on 19 December 2005 at the K-1 World Grand Prix in Tokyo. With just Edwin van Os in his corner, he managed to give Leko a dose of his own medicine by knocking out Leko in the second round with a spinning kick to the head. This was the start of a lucrative career in the K-1 that lasted eight years, but never got him the title. He did come very close in 2009 when he lost by KO in the final match against Sem Schilt.

THE PRODIGAL SON RETURNS

A year after Badr left me I received a telephone call. "Hey Sen, this is Badr. Could we have a talk?" I said: "Drop by the gym". I didn't want him in my house, after all that had happened. This was after he had broken his jaw in Australia after falling victim to a rolling thunder kick by Peter Graham. Badr said to me that he wanted to come back. I said: "That's fine, son. Everybody is allowed a mistake in their life. I'm glad you're back." I really meant that. It was pretty emotional, we both shed some tears.

He started training the next day. It was a Monday evening. I usually leave after I'm done teaching, but the lads will often go into the sauna. So the entire competition group including Amir Zeyada, Hesdy Gerges and Menno Dijkstra went into the sauna. In the sauna Badr said: "Boy, I've really missed this, those hard workouts. It feels great to be back." The next day he attended my morning class at 10am. Afterwards he went into the sauna again. When he came out of the sauna he bumped into an individual we'll be calling "Bob" [not his real name], who was a prominent member of the Amsterdam chapter of the Hells Angels. Both of them jumped when they saw each other. After this incident, Badr didn't return to the gym and neither did Bob. I later learnt there was a big problem between the two of them as Badr had screwed Bob's girlfriend. After he stayed away for several days everyone said: "I thought Badr was back." I don't phone students when they don't attend class and I never have. "Uncle" Henk, my assistant and bar man in the gym, decided to give Badr a ring to ask him why he hadn't returned to the gym. "I'll explain it to you some day, Henkie," Badr told him. This was the second time he left my gym. It was almost two years after his second departure that I heard about Badr's problem with Bob. Both of them were frightened. Had I known about the problem earlier on I could have had a talk with the two of them and said: "What you do outside of the gym is none of my business, but I won't have trouble in the gym." In that way the whole thing could have been resolved.

The weakest thing about Badr is that he only thinks about saving his own ass. Leaving my gym, shouting: "He stole money from me", and then returning after a year and then staying away again after two classes because of a private matter. The Hells Angels decided that Badr wasn't allowed to fight in the Netherlands for a year due to his conflict with Bob. And so it went. The Hells Angels do have that power.

I spoke to a lot of Moroccan people about it and they told me: "If only he had stayed under your tutelage, Mr. Harinck, he wouldn't have resorted to foul play and would have become the K-1 champ." When he trained under me he was 86 kg and of course people get heavier as they age, especially when they're in their twenties. But one and a half years later Badr weighed 112 kg and it certainly wasn't body fat that he gained. I think it's highly unlikely that he could make such a dramatic physical transformation by consuming only broiled chicken breasts and steamed broccoli. If you take extracurricular supplements to be stronger, it messes up your mind. You lose your grip on reality. In August 2013 it was confirmed what I had known all along. A wide range of doping was found in Badr's fridge when the police raided his house, including anapolon, which is one of the strongest illegal steroids out there.

In the K-1 finals in Japan in 2008, Badr first won a clear victory over Peter Aerts. When matched against Remy Bonjasky and he found himself unable to get a grip on the match, Badr went completely berserk. When Remy was lying on the ground, Badr punched him twice and stomped on his face. With this behaviour he disgraced the K-1, the sport of kickboxing and above all himself.

At this point everyone in the Netherlands knows who Badr is, but that's more due to his negative behaviour than anything else. He hasn't fought an opponent of any importance in the last two years. He won his second match against Alexei Ignashov, but let's face it, Ignashov is an old wino and of no importance in the top of the world. I think he won't be able to hold himself against any of the real top heavyweight fighters. There's no lack of talent here, but hard work is irreplaceable and if you're not willing to train, you'll get nowhere.

Badr was in a relationship with Estelle Gullit [ex-wife of former soccer international Ruud Gullit] for a few years and she is a very wealthy lady. The consequence was that Badr became complacent. A fighter training for a match should be busting his butt in the gym, training should be the only thing he thinks about. The higher the prosperity of the fighter, the lower the results in the ring. It's a law of nature.

In all honesty, I don't think I would have been able to discipline Badr had he stayed with me. When I trained him he was still a bit younger. In your late teens you'll have respect for Thom Harinck, but at 24-25 you'll likely go your own way. The problem was and is the entourage of people who are always kissing Badr's ass. Everything Badr says is the truth and nothing but the truth. At some point this kid thinks: I can get away with anything, I am the king of the castle. But there's a side of society that doesn't accept this behaviour: the law, the police, the public prosecutor. Since he left my gym, nobody could discipline him. Not Andre Mannaart, Edwin van Os or Mike Passenier. They were glad when he came walking in, because a trainer gets part of the prize money. Badr is a money making machine. I was the only trainer who told him how it was. With me he had to shut up, train and behave in a responsible way.

There were sometimes problems. When he was depressed because his girlfriend left him, I gave him a pep talk. When he did something wrong, I told him off. He missed that. I was the only one. He can use his big mouth and show off all he wants. Deep in his heart he knows the truth. He was always welcome in my house, I was always correct towards him, I never took a cent more than was agreed upon, and he dined with my family. My wife helped his mother several times by writing letters for her.

He's simply brainwashed by hangers-on who think that everything he does is OK. It drives one mad. You could see the same thing with Johan Cruijff, everybody was always kissing his ass. You might be a top soccer player, that doesn't necessarily make you a good human being, or mean you know everything. You must be aware of your limits. I have my good and bad characteristics. If you always get your way and are never corrected, bad will come of it sooner or later. Badr is the ideal case for a psychologist. If Badr had had someone to steer him away from bad people, told him what was good and bad, and have him concentrate on his fighting career, he would have achieved way more. It's a great pity. I mean, Badr is a professional fighter, it's his livelihood, so why not give it your all?

The question: Why did you leave Thom Harinck? is a question Badr has heard countless times. Older and wiser Moroccan men told me: "I did tell him not to leave". But Badr just shrugged his shoulders. They all knew that he won nearly all his matches when I was his coach and that he also behaved normally. Life gives you what you deserve. I would much rather have seen him winning the K-1 than having to see him sitting in court with eight counts of violent behaviour against him. "The former pupil of Thom Harinck" is a label he will never lose, whether Badr likes it or not. I know it frustrates him. In a recent talk show on Moroccan television, Badr was interviewed. When they asked him, "Wasn't Thom Harinck your first trainer?" Badr said: "That man knows nothing. Mike Passenier is ten times better." He makes a fool of himself by saying things like that. You learn things from every coach. Every coach has his strong and weak points, just like a fighter does. Saying that I don't know anything, while there isn't a coach to be found who produced as many world champions as I did is childish behaviour. He could have said something like: "He gave me my base".

In the biography Badr dictated, he pisses on everyone. He says that Ernesto Hoost wanted a fixed match when Ernesto Hoost would never do a thing like that. If that's the way you have to profile yourself, you're worthless in my eyes.

CHAMPIONS 2000-2014

HESDY "FIGHTER'S HEART" GERGES

When Hesdy came to me he was working as a construction worker. He had trained in Hoofddorp under Bolem Belaini, a former pupil of mine. Belaini said to me: "Sensei, I have a guy with talent. He should go to your gym." And so that's what happened. He was physically strong but couldn't do all that much. In the beginning he not only got beatings from Badr, but also from all of the other guys. When Hesdy started in my gym, Badr was already champion of the Netherlands. Badr used Hesdy as his personal punching bag, so much that I had to intervene on several occasions. When Badr left my gym, Hesdy was only in the C-category and I told him: "I'll make a new champion out of you." I was right. He didn't have Badr's talent. He continued coming to the gym, I thought by myself: He has character. That's how he got his nickname "Fighter's heart". Early on he fought a few matches and often got a beating, but fought back simply because of that character. He progressed from Dutch champion to champion of the Benelux and subsequently to European champion. He made his name by fighting against Ruslan

Karaev in a tournament organised by Glory. Karaev got a terrible beating; Hesdy was in excellent shape that day.

His international breakthrough was in a match against Sem Schilt. I was in Japan for the K-1 World Grand Prix 2009 and Ishii said: "Sem Schilt's opponent isn't coming. Do you have anyone, preferably a heavyweight who is not a Dutchman?" "Sure, no problem", I said and picked up my phone. I told Hesdy to come to Japan on the first flight available. Hesdy's father is an Egyptian and Hesdy has a double nationality, so he could represent Egypt at the tournament.

GINTY VREDE (1985-2008)

My student Hesdy Gerges fought a match against Ginty Vrede on 3 December 2007 in Utrecht. The first round was a tie with perhaps a light advantage for Ginty. But with 20 seconds to go in the first round, Ginty started a slug fest that left Hesdy lying on the canvas after receiving a terrible haymaker. Ginty was coached by Harry Berenpoot of Bear Paw's Gym. Ginty was not that well known as a fighter, but we had heard that he was a talented young man. If you fight against a guy that's better known than you and you win, you become better known, that's how it goes. So Ginty made quite a name for himself by knocking out Hesdy. He later fought in the US and became world champion in muay thai with the World Boxing Council, knocking out Shane Del Rosario, again in the first round.

I liked to compare Ginty to Frank Lobman, a famous fighter from the pioneering days in the Netherlands. Frank Lobman was a champion in both kyokushinkai karate and kickboxing. He was originally from Suriname and lived in Rotterdam. He was as strong as a bear and won almost all his fights by knockout.

I went to the gym to teach my evening class on Monday 28 January 2008 when Ginty walked in with his girlfriend. He was a very polite and calm young man. "Sensei, could I join your class?" He was already familiar with gym etiquette. I said: "Sure, no problem". He told me: "I've just come from a party and I've hung around town." Later we learnt that he hadn't slept for 24 hours and hadn't eaten anything all day. It was 5pm and my class didn't start until 7pm. So he sat at the bar and socialized, which he was very good at. He was drinking one Red Bull after another. I jokingly said to him: "Son, that Red Bull is poison, it'll give you a heart attack." He replied: "No problem man, I can take it."

When my class started we began with a vigorous warm-up with skipping rope in the standard chakuriki style. Then we started sparring. I first put him against one of the boys, he sparred as was required. Then I put him against another boy, same story. Then he sparred Hesdy. I said to them beforehand: "Guys, we'll be keeping this clean, OK?" "Oesh, sensei." But from the first second they were killing each other. I interrupted them and said to them both: "This is your final warning, we're keeping this clean. This is not a match, we're just sparring. You can go full-contact on the body, but just tap the head". "Oesh, sensei." Ginty had a tough cookie in Hesdy. I thought: Good sparring experience for Hesdy. The round after that he sparred Ginty again. Again, they went at it pretty hard. Hesdy wanted to show him that Hesdy's earlier knockout was due to a lucky punch. Well, actually there are no lucky punches, as a punch is just a punch.

Hesdy was scoring his points with kicks and punches. Suddenly Ginty waved his hand, signifying he wanted to stop sparring. I asked him: "What's the matter?" He said: "I'm not feeling well." He turned as pale as a ghost. I sponged his head with some cold water and asked: "How do you feel?" "Not too good," he replied. Then he lay down on the ground. I was training some 20 guys and I immediately said: "Everyone out of the room. Call for an ambulance." I opened the nearest door to the ring to let some fresh air in. I had a restaurant owner and a police officer in the competition group who both knew how to resuscitate people. They tried in turns until the ambulance arrived. The medic also tried, but it didn't seem to work. They carried him into the ambulance. He passed away on his way to the hospital.

It's a strange experience that a guy who knocks out one of your students comes to your gym to spar and it turns out to be the last thing he does. Ginty's mother and girlfriend visited the gym after his passing away. We attended the funeral with a bunch of guys from the gym and it was a very impressive funeral with all those mourners in the training suits of their respective gyms. Ginty Vrede was only 22 years old.

HESDY GERGES VS SEM SCHILT (28 March 2009)

The first time Hesdy fought Sem Schilt was in Yokohama, Japan. In the first round Hesdy got a terrible beating with Schilt scoring with his deadly jabs and front kicks. Many an opponent found himself in dreamland after being on the receiving end. Hesdy scored quite a bit with blows to the head but got an eight count after one of Schilt's knees connected in the second round. After three rounds Schilt was declared the winner, but the Japanese public got to respect Hesdy for flying in at a few days notice and fighting an opponent for whom he wasn't prepared.

When Hesdy fought Schilt the second time, Hesdy scored with low-kicks several times, while Schilt connected with jabs and a knee to the head. In the third round Schilt almost got KO'd on the legs. The match ended as a loss for Hesdy. Through hard work, by being a so-called gym rat, he now ranks in the top 10 of the world. He is currently rated 5 by Glory, one of the most important organisations after the demise of the K-1. His low-kicks are very hard. He's very fast; an aspect I trained a lot with him.

BADR HARI VS HESDY GERGES (29 May 2010)

It was only a question of time before the two top heavyweights, Badr and Hesdy, would face each other in the ring. The fight was scheduled as the main fight at Simon Rutz' yearly event in Amsterdam Arena. When the fight started many people in the crowd thought the fight wouldn't last beyond the first round. Badr scored with murderous hooks that seemed to come straight from the Mike Tyson textbook. Badr hit Hesdy in the head, while Hesdy scored with kicks to the ribs, but it didn't seem to bother Badr at all. The second round began with a slugfest. Badr, though, seemed tired and looked like he had spent all his energy. After 40 seconds, Hesdy slipped to the ground, when he tried to get up with his knees still on the ground, Badr delivered an illegal kick to Hesdy's temple. The public was booing while Hesdy was rolling on the canvas. In the meanwhile, referee Joop Ubeda disqualified Badr. Melvin Manhoef, who was there to assist Mike Passenier, came to our corner to apologize. Hesdy walked over to Badr's corner and only after several attempts did Badr respond and give him a hug. Badr and his team walked out of the ring before the prize giving.

After this foul play you could see Mike Passenier wiping the snot from Badr's nose with his forefinger. Badr spoiled the event, got himself suspended and brought bad publicity to the sport. He deserved a clip around the ear and I as a coach would have given him one. A fighter won't do anything back, because he knows you're right. Mike's behaviour shows that he doesn't have the upper hand on Badr and without that you won't ever be successful. A fighter should respect his trainer. I wouldn't have accepted this type of behaviour. Badr didn't even apologize, you can see in the footage from the match that he's just sheepishly staring through his dilated pupils.

Hesdy was able to withstand Badr due to the gruelling workouts. I let him spar with three men in the ring: Jérôme Le Banner, Peter Aerts and Amir Zeyada. He got a terrible beating. At one point his cheek was so swollen that I had to tell the guys to only hit him on the body. Hesdy later said: "Sen, the blows I received in the gym were harder than those I got from Badr." Mentally he was super sharp. I impressed on him how good Badr was and how he could catch people off guard. I told him beforehand everything what Badr would do and it all came out. Later Badr would say: "I was fighting Thom Harinck."

SATOSHI ISHII

Satoshi Ishii came to my gym in 2013. He had already won an Olympic gold medal in judo at the Olympic Summer Games in Beijing in 2008, and got involved in MMA after that. He came to me to improve his standing fight game. He fought two matches in the period that he trained under me and won them both. I once had him as our opponent when he fought an MMA-match against Jérôme le Banner. Jérôme lost the match. After that, Satoshi came to me. To date he has fought 18 MMA matches of which he won 13. He trained quite a bit with UFC-heavyweight fighter Gegard Mousasi after I quit teaching.

He is a mild-natured, well-mannered and sweet man. Most of the Japanese are ideal students if they come and train under you. Discipline is their middle name. He was also very courteous. I had no problem coaching him in a MMA-match. I have done it several times before, with Jérôme Le Banner and others. When the worldwide MMA-explosion took place halfway through the 1990s with organisations like Pride and UFC, I was training the top kickboxers. That was the reason I didn't switch to MMA. But chakuriki is an all-round fighting style. And coaching is coaching, whether it's a K-1 or a MMA match.

JÉRÔME LE BANNER

I trained Jérôme Le Banner for about two years during the last phase of his career. He came to me after a loss against Sem Schilt in which he was knocked out after 45 seconds. He would come over from France for two to three months at a time before his match. He would hire a house or apartment, or would sometimes stay in a hotel, but often it would be a house. He wasn't exactly poor and could easily afford it. He deals in real estate in France with a couple of mates. Fighting for him is more a hobby as he doesn't actually need to earn any money from it. I found him to be very willing to learn as a student.

I remember one time he came too late for class. I looked at him very angrily. He had to do 50 push-ups as a punishment. I had a group training session with Peter Aerts, Raul Catinas and Frank Munoz among the students. Later that day he was at my house for drinks and he told my wife: "I was afraid of Thom today, the way he looked at me." This sounded funny coming from a champion in his early forties. But in the gym, I'm the sensei, I can't distinguish between beginners and seasoned champions. He won all of his matches in his two years with me. His wins under my guidance included a match against Tyrone Spong in 2010. He also won a fight against Stefan Leko for the world title in free-style kickboxing in Switzerland in 2011.

There is a pattern where students return to a coach after trying to do it on their own. Peter Aerts returned to me after his loss against Badr Hari in 2008. After that he defeated Gokhan Saki and Sem Schilt. At some point, many fighters reach a certain level that they think they can do it all without a coach in their corner. If they think: I'm going to do 50 push-ups, and when they reach the 48th rep, they think: I'm tired, so I'll quit. A coach would make them squeeze out those last two reps. It's not that a fighter who trains himself is doomed to be unsuccessful, far from it. I have authority over the fighters, that's my task. I will push a student that tiny little bit extra that he wouldn't do by himself or with a friend that trains him. I am not a fighter's friend, I'm the coach. I'm above them, at least in the gym.

The fighter in the ring has to do the job, but it's approximately 70 per cent of the whole endeavour. The coach is the remaining 30 per cent. The coach will give instructions during the match and tell him what tactics to follow in the rest period. He has to mentally pull him through if the fighter is in physical pain. Sometimes a fighter thinks: I won't make it. Then the coach has to motivate him.

This happened twice with Badr Hari: in his fight against Antoni Hardonk, where he didn't want to continue after the fourth round, and in his fight against Errol Paris where he wanted to call the fight off beforehand. In both cases I pulled him through. Badr ended up winning both matches. Top fighters realise that the coach is 30 per cent of their success, that's why they come looking for me. A good mental coach is of the utmost importance if a top fighter wants to fight at full capacity.

MENNO "THE MACHINE GUN" DIJKSTRA

Menno Dijkstra first came walking into my gym as a 15-year-old boy from Amstelveen, hand in hand with his mother. He was very unsure of himself. Like every mother, his mother was worried. "Will he be hit on the head?" she asked. I assured her: "I have kids myself. I know it's not a good thing to get hit on the head. We try to avoid it. But it is a hard gym, we are known for our tough training systems." I had never expected that the boy that walked into my gym hand in hand with his mother would develop into a rugged fighter. He was not a street kid and came from a respectable family. But, he had determination and a fighter's heart. I thought it was unbelievable. He became Dutch champion, European Champion and fought for the world title and won. He became friends with Milco Lambrecht (the man behind the *RINGS Holland* organisation) and helped him promote several events. He assisted me with giving seminars in the favelas in Brazil in 2014. I thought, if he performs his task well, he will be rewarded. I planned it beforehand and after the seminars I awarded him a black belt and teacher certificate in the chakuriki style.

AMIR ZEYADA

Amir Zeyada has an Egyptian father and a Dutch mother. He came to me when he was 12, while his little brother came to me when he was only four and couldn't speak any Dutch. Amir became best friends with Menno Dijkstra. Amir has an impressive physique, and equal fighting spirit. He's a fighter that either wins by knockout, or loses by knockout. He always stayed loyal to the Chakuriki Gym. Some fighters go shopping from one gym to another. Amir fought 73 matches. After a short stint at Mike's Gym, where he couldn't find what he was looking for, he is now fighting for Pancration again. One time he had to fight and I couldn't go with him and he was sick about it. The whole family fights, his sister was one of my competition fighters. His brother used to fight, but doesn't fight anymore because he is busy studying. His father worked for several kickboxing organisations. It's a family of fighters. I am currently organising a match for Amir. He still wants to fight a few matches before ending his career. He's a Chakuriki-man in heart and soul. Outside of the ring he's a polite and quiet young man.

RETIREMENT AND THE FUTURE

THE END OF COACHING

I was in Zagreb for Hesdy Gerges' match against Ismael Londt at the K-1 World Grand Prix of 2013. Gerges didn't fight as well as he usually does – he was a bit too static. He scored more in the second round, but received several knees to his head. He had a cut on his face. After the end of the round, he told me he couldn't see anymore as the blood was flowing into his eyes. I told him to quit; you have to be able to see clearly if you want to be able to defend yourself. On a sunny April morning, a week later I was walking to the gym. Hesdy was free, but a few of the other guys had fights coming up. I suddenly noticed I didn't feel like going. I just didn't feel like it. That was for the first time in 42 years! That evening I said to my wife: "I'm going to quit.." "You're going to quit?" she asked a bit startled. I answered: "Yes, I'm going to quit. I'm no longer motivated, I don't feel like it anymore. I will tell my boys about it."

The next day, I was at the gym at our regular training time of 10am. There were 12 guys, including Frank Munoz and Amir Zeyada. Amir is 28 and has been trained by me since he was a 12-year-old boy. When I told them I wanted to quit they couldn't believe their ears. They said: "But why, Sen? Is there a problem?" I said: "There's no problem, I'm just through with it." After my last lesson I gave them all a handshake and a hug, I went home and that was the end of it. It was reported on Twitter and the martial arts forums and soon everybody knew that I had quit coaching.

Shortly thereafter, at a martial arts event in the north of Amsterdam hosted by Chris Dolman and his daughter Sharon, I was awarded the title "Grandmaster in Free-fight" with a certificate. At a RINGS Holland event in Amstelveen I was given a beautiful belt by Patrik Eriksson and Menno Dijkstra, two fighters I had coached to championship titles. The competition group bought me a Rolex. I'm not that fond of brands, but it's a beautiful watch and the newest model. I really appreciated the gesture, I hadn't expected it.

Will I completely end my involvement with kickboxing? That's not my intention. I also want to write a book about coaching. I would resume work for a kickboxing organization, on the condition that the organization gets recognized by the government. We recently had a gathering in Amsterdam with about 100 people involved in the sport of kickboxing together with the mayors of Amsterdam and Hoorn. The goal was to coordinate the sport that has been linked to criminality and suffers from confusion due to the many different organizations active in the sport: up to 30! There had also been a shooting at a kickboxing event in Hoorn in 2012. Nowadays people can get kicked to death at soccer matches or in fights outside, so it's more a problem of society as a whole, not just of the martial arts. I would accept a position as leader or adviser for such an organization. So, I won't be completely saying *sayonara* to the sport, I love it too much for that. For many people, my retirement came kind of suddenly. But never in my life have I done something that I didn't enjoy and now is no time to start. From Brazil and Japan, I got invitations to come to events that would celebrate my retirement from the sport. I politely declined – I wouldn't travel that far if it wasn't for a fight.

What people don't realize is that when a fighter fights abroad, the coach accompanies him, which means you're gone for four to five days. If you go to Japan, you have an incredibly long flight and then you have the heat and you have to sit around for hours. My wife has a good job, she's professor in Law at the Free University of Amsterdam and does several other tasks on the side. I also have three young children who need my attention. I just don't feel like leaving home any more six to seven times a year for eight days every time.

During the last two to three years, it often happened that guys who have fought a match didn't get paid. All my boys still have to receive their prize money from an event held in December 2012. The money is always transferred to the bank account of the fighter. My fighters approach me and say: "Sen, could you give that promoter a ring or shoot him an email, I still haven't received my prize money." There are even fighters who fought in the K-1's New Year 's Eve event of 2011 in the Saitama Super Arena in Japan, organized by Antonio Inoki, who still haven't been paid. Jérôme Le Banner, for instance. So the level of the sport is moving upwards, while financially it's moving downwards, with the exception of a few events where a lot of money can be earned. There's no progress regarding the majority of events for professional fighters. These events are broadcast and the promoters earn lots of money by selling the television rights. This is belittling towards the fighters.

When Gilbert Ballantine and Peter Aerts trained at my gym we got 10,000 euros for a match. That was even before television involvement, with hardly any sponsors. Now it's broadcast in 130 countries and the television rights are sold for considerable amounts for each country. Fighters who have been fighting for many years can earn 5,000 euros for a match. The fighters are earning less and less, and the promoters are getting filthy rich. This is something that doesn't appeal to me. It's something you can't influence as a fighter or trainer. These promoters can do whatever they want, as the process isn't coordinated by a separate commission like the Nevada Athletic Commission in the US. We will never reach the maturity in kickboxing they have in boxing, where a world champion receives $10 million for a championship match that is broadcast on TV. Mike Tyson has fought matches for $40 million in the past. A top kickboxer will earn $40,000 to 50,000 for a match. There isn't a level playing field, it just isn't fair.

Since the demise of the K-1, the organization called Glory is doing well. But Glory is reorganizing and the fees that fighters were paid at the beginning have been falling. Jérôme Le Banner told me that for the last few Glory events, fighters have been paid less and less. They entice fighters to fight for their organization by promising them nice sums at the start. I understand that a promoter and his team should be paid for their work, but it shouldn't be to the detriment of the fighters. That's another reason for quitting coaching; I don't want to be a part of a situation in which fighters are paid less and less, or not at all.

There's a new competition format that I'm planning on introducing, but only if I get a contract for it to be broadcast on television. I could do that for the next 20 years. My 70th birthday has passed and I plan to live to at least 110 years old, so I still have a few decades left!

AN OFFER FROM THE USA

About a month before I retired from teaching, I got an offer from Florida, USA. The offer was from a very wealthy man who sponsored a kickboxing team. He made me an offer to come to the US for a year. He had selected ten young men who would be trained by me. I would be paid very well. They had a gym and an apartment ready for me. I liked the idea but told him I would have to take my wife and children with me. That wasn't possible. He said: "You have to take care of your family yourself." My wife is busy teaching and is a member of several commissions, and all my kids are in high school. It would be impractical to take them away for a year. I offered to train the young men in the Netherlands, which would be even better, as they would have experienced sparring partners to train with. That wasn't possible either, so the whole deal was off. There was a lot of money involved; several hundred thousands of dollars. My family is more important to me than money. However, it was a challenge which I would have liked to have taken on. The guy said the ten Americans were pretty good and talented, although we should probably take that with a pinch of salt. I've often heard Americans say this during my trips to the States and in reality the Americans have turned out to be less than spectacular. But if I had had ten guys, I would probably have made a champion out of at least one or two of them.

THE ENGLISHMAN THAT DRANK TOO MUCH

In 2014 I was on a trip to Brazil with my student Menno Dijkstra. It's a 12-hour flight and we had both taken a sleeping pill. An object hit me and some commotion woke me from my sleep. There was an Englishman who had been drinking heavily and was asking for more liquor. The stewardesses didn't want to give him any and he went berserk. He was standing and shouting. The purser was called in and he seemed to be a very nice guy, but not quite the type to subdue an English hooligan. I saw that the purser was getting into trouble. All the other people in the plane were too scared to do anything. The English guy was with a bunch of friends, but luckily his friends didn't get involved. I dived over Menno and gave the Englishman a right cross on the chin. The Englishman was out for a little while. This gave us the chance to handcuff his hands behind his back. We placed him on one of the seats that the stewardesses use. I wanted to go back to sleep in my seat, but after five minutes, he began making trouble again. He was shouting and kicking against the wall with his feet. I went to him and said in English: "Fuck off! You don't have to behave like an imbecile. If you make any more trouble I'll let my elbow shoot out. So just shut up!" I used street language in the hope I could get through to him and it worked. He stayed quiet for the remainder of the flight.

When we arrived at Schiphol airport, we all had to stay seated while the military police came aboard. They took the Englishman with them and we could only leave the plane after he had been taken away. The stewardess approached me and gave me two gift vouchers of 50 euros with the text: "Thanks for your help, Mr. Harinck". They very much appreciated what I had done, but I just saw it as my duty. Nobody else did anything. What would have happened if the guy had gone totally berserk? You can't call the pilot, because he has to fly the aeroplane. I just did what was right. The incident was reported in several magazines. The funniest thing about it was that Menno slept through the whole thing. When he woke up I said: "Menno, your sensei just had to fight!" "What?", he asked in amazement. "You should have woken me up!"

HOW MANY DEGREES?

I have black belt degrees in kempo, jiu-jitsu and wushu. I also have a sixth degree in kyokushinkai karate. Added together, all the degrees would make a couple of dozen. All these degrees are honorary in nature. It's customary in the Orient that masters or leaders of an organisation award degrees to people they respect or consider legends. That doesn't mean that I know all of the material that these masters know who presented me with these ranks. Nor does it necessarily mean that I as an individual am associated with the styles that they teach. You won't see me teaching or performing the elaborate forms of the Chinese martial arts, and that's OK, since they aren't my cup of tea anyway. I truly appreciate all of the awards and degrees. Some of them are from masters from China. Those masters may be very well known over there, but are for the most part completely unknown in the West. When you meet them at an event, you're awarded a 4th, 5th or 6th degree as a pat on the back for advancing the martial arts.

FUTURE PROJECTS

There was a program on television in which school kids could say something about their school teachers. And it was: "cancer" this and "cancer" that, and "that motherfucker". The word "cancer" is used as an abusive adjective in Dutch slang. I tweeted: "They wouldn't have said that in my presence." The next day the doorbell rang and there was a movie crew standing before my front door. "What's your opinion on this?" they asked. I said: "That young man who uses 'cancer' as every other word. Let him work for two months in the Emma Children's Hospital, in the cancer ward. And then we'll see if he ever uses the word 'cancer' again."

I got boatloads of reactions from people who said: "Finally there's someone who opens his mouth about this." Those street punks have nothing on me. I notice that many of the youths of today don't have any respect. And the people who want to teach them respect are afraid to do it.

In fact, I might be playing a role in a reality TV series called Tuigjeugd (Rough Kids). The idea of the series is to approach street kids and teach them a bit of respect. They preferred me as a presenter above the seasoned TV presenter Arie Boomsma who is an incredibly big guy. The cameraman was taking some shots from a distance while I was having a discussion with the presenter. My dog, in his youthful enthusiasm, knocked down the camera man. That bit of footage can be found on the internet and has got more than 100,000 hits on YouTube!

ONE OF THE HAPPIEST PEOPLE ON THE PLANET

I was lucky enough to be able to turn my passion into my profession, and was successful at it. It never made me really rich, but that's OK. I have a wonderful family. I'm married to a beautiful, young, intelligent lady who I am still very much in love with. I have three wonderful children. All three of them play hockey and all three of them play an instrument. What more could a man wish for? At the age of 71 I'm in good health. If I look around me, I see people my age getting cancer or dying. So I'm one of the happiest people on the planet. I go to the gym every morning on weekdays. I do 45 minutes of weights, rope jumping and bag work. I reserve the weekends for my family.

WHAT MAKES IT ALL WORTHWHILE

I bump into quite a few people. If I go on the ferry from the north of Amsterdam to the city centre, people suddenly say to me: "Oesh, sensei. How are you?" It might be an older Moroccan, a Surinamese or a Dutch man who says this. I always answer and return the question, though sometimes I don't even recognize them. Then I think to myself: Who was that again? And when I talk to them I find out. People often say: "Thanks to my training in the chakuriki style I got through rough periods."

I once spoke to a former student who had to serve a few years in prison. He was able to look after himself in jail where there is a sort of pecking order. Another guy lost his wife and said that he turned to the Zen meditation I taught him to overcome his grief. As a result of the discipline that I teach, many students have been able to withstand the temptations of the criminal path. That's what makes it all worthwhile for me, that they understood the essence of the chakuriki style.

POSTSCRIPT

In 2016 Thom Harinck picked up coaching. He trained a single student, Hesdy Gerges, every weekday. In early 2018 Hesdy Gerges chose to switch to Mousid Gym in Amsterdam.

BONUS CHAPTER: MONDO (QUESTIONS AND ANSWERS)

Any tips for quicker recovery after intensive training?

Recovery is very important. It's impossible to draw up charts for how much rest an athlete needs after intensive training. Every human being is unique. Every body will react differently.

As a trainer, I was gifted with the foresight to sense when a pupil needed rest. I could see it in the way they moved, I would look them in the eyes and if the white was extended I would say: "You're tired, aren't you?" They would answer: "Yes." Then I would say: "You won't be training tonight, go and get some rest." Scientists always want to predict stuff like this through charts and formulas. A good coach should sense this. I would say to my students: "If you're tired, tell me. Don't train, as you'll only get injuries and gain nothing."

As an athlete you should listen to your body, get plenty of sleep and the majority of calories that you consume should come from unprocessed natural foods. Getting a massage – if you can afford it – will help, taking a nap if your schedule allows it won't hurt and spending time in an infrared sauna (if your gym has one) is recommended.

Is there a certain way to psych up a pupil before a fight?

Yes, but it doesn't only happen before a fight, it happens during the training as well. That's why one-on-one coaching is so important in an individual sport. A soccer coach has 11 guys running around the field and a few reserves. In the martial arts, the relationship between athlete and coach is way more intense. During the training you're trying to harden your pupil mentally, trying to pull him through the difficult moments. It is during the match that the climax of that training should be reached. It may happen that in between rounds, a fighter wants to give up. You can say certain things to the fighter that enables him to continue and maybe even win the match. This too is something you should sense as a coach, and is something you can't find in books. If you train an individual for several years, you know his or her weak points.

For instance, Badr Hari can't tolerate pain very well. If his opponent inflicts pain on him, he panics and often resorts to unsportsmanlike behaviour. If everything goes his way, he is a sublime fighter. Peter Aerts is the opposite. He needs a few punches and kicks to wake him up and start brawling. Just like you can increase an athlete's endurance, so you can also increase his mental toughness to peak during the match, and the coach should be present to pull him through any rough territory.

What should a fighter do for a good endurance next to the regular kickboxing classes?

An all-round kickboxing training should be of primary importance. It should contain tactical training, strength training, technique training, stretching and endurance training. The mental side should also be included. It sounds like the questioner only trains techniques in his gym. You can make it as all-round as you wish as a fighter, but your coach ought to know what you're up to. There was a time when I coached everything myself: the running, the weight training, a fighter's diet and so forth. I would also act as the manager and often organise the event at which they would fight. When the sport professionalised, fighters would seek out a weight trainer, a conditioning coach etc. I'm not a big supporter of this but this is the choice of the fighter and I would allow it. But, they had to tell me exactly what they'd done. I had to tailor my training to that. If a conditioning coach has left you gasping for air, while lying in a puddle of your own sweat in the gym in the morning, I wouldn't be doing the same in the evening.

A kickboxing training that includes all facets of fighting should be of primary importance. If you want to do weights on the side, don't fall for a heavy bodybuilding style. High reps with low weights will help develop muscular endurance. A professional trainer should be able to help you with that, and make sure an athlete doesn't overtrain. So to recap: make sure you're taking classes that include all aspects of kickboxing, before you add anything else.

Tips for losing weight before a match?

There are guys whose weight can differ 7 to 8 kilos between the day of the weighing and the day of the fight. They take a pee-pill, which I am strongly opposed to because you lose all the fluids in your body. And we all know that an athlete should be well hydrated if he wants to perform at his peak. Most times you know about two to three months beforehand when your pupil has to fight. If you can make that weight naturally, you should choose a gradual approach. It should be a realistic goal. It may be that the pupil is completely shredded at his current weight, in which case it's a bad idea. Say you weigh 55 kilos and the fight weight is 50 kilos. You should set a weekly goal of losing a certain amount of grams. Losing weight very quickly diminishes your strength. I've seen young men who are 78 kilos one day, and the next day they weigh in at 72 kilos. The weighing always takes place the day before the match. Then they start eating and drinking quickly and fight at around 75 kilos. But I was never a proponent of this way of "cutting" as they call it in bodybuilding circles. I like stability. Extreme measures often lead to extreme disappointments. It's also bad for the mental side. It will only make a fighter more anxious. "Will I be able to make my weight?" will be running through his mind.

When I organised events in the past, I saw guys from other gyms jumping rope for half an hour before the weigh-in, to get the last half kilo off. Before that, they had been in the sauna for an hour. That is the wrong approach. So to recap: only lose weight when the goal is realistic and take a gradual approach.

If I'm on vacation in Thailand and want to fight a match, what would you advise me to do?

It often happens that tourists fight in a bar. They won't let you fight in the Rajadamnern or Lumpinee stadiums out of the blue. You'll see this quite a lot in the bars in Pattaya where the prostitutes tend to congregate. There will be a small Thai man, and an announcer will shout something like: "10,000 *bath* for the guy who can beat our fighter!" Often Americans or guys from other countries have been drinking and want to impress the ladies.

I've seen countless *farang* [foreigners] having the living daylights beaten out of them this way. Only a few times was there a trained individual from the Netherlands who stood a chance. Determine who your opponent is beforehand and focus on boxing, since the Thai fighter will be kicking a lot. I'm not a big supporter of this, it's comparable to fighting at traveling fairs and I don't like that practice very much.

I strongly advise against fighting your first match in Thailand. Even if you've fought five matches you will hardly stand a chance. Often the Thai fighters in the ring are former champions. Sometimes they are caught on a lee shore and need an income. Overall they are pretty good and experienced fighters. They're there every night. Often the referees will help them a bit. I would advise everyone to think twice before stepping into a Thai ring. It's way better to have your coach back home fix you a fight against someone of approximately the same skill and experience with an organisation that you're familiar with.

If a beginner starts training in kickboxing he won't start training 12 times a week. How could one build this up?

Most people start with twice a week. After some time, if you see as a coach that they have an interest and show character, I would say: "Come for one extra session starting next week." This too you should build up gradually. These are all things a good coach should guide. There are many excellent kickboxing coaches in the Netherlands, but at the same time, there are many coaches who hardly know what they're doing and have zero education.

There is no governing body to regulate the sport, which means that certain individuals who can just about pronounce the words "low-kick" and "left hook" are teaching classes, sometimes even in commercial gyms. The bottom line is to build it up gradually. If you're new to the sport, don't start by training seven days a week. That won't work. If you train every day, vary what you do during the week. Focus on weight training on one day, endurance on another and flexibility on the next.

How and what should one eat on the day of the competition?

I always use the analogy of a hunter who's out for prey. If he has a full stomach, he won't be as mobile and as eager to find his prey. With fighting it's exactly the same. You should eat your last meal at least four or five hours beforehand. It is common knowledge that it takes approximately three hours to digest a meal. On the day of the match fighters are often anxious which affects the speed of digestion.

So I always tell my students to eat a good breakfast after they wake up. Most fights will take place in the evening. Between 1 and 2pm you can eat a calorie-heavy meal with foods like pasta. This will be after the weigh-in. After that only fruit, like an apple or a banana. The fruit will give you energy, keep you from becoming too hungry and will digest quickly. You often see fighters at kickboxing events with a bunch of bananas in their sports bag. Remember to take small bites and chew well, which aids digestion. Make sure not to have several platefuls of food in your stomach before any fighting competition.

I've seen you teach classes in which you use intervals and shout "Chico" at the end. What's the theory behind that?

There are several reasons. In the first place, you'll get pretty tired at the end of a three-minute-round. I let the fighter know how long he still has to go, so he can adjust his endurance accordingly. I also use the word "Chico" when teaching in the gym. If I shout "Chico" the student should squeeze out the last bit of willpower that's left in his body. The last 30 seconds of a match always remain the most vivid in the memory of the judges. If the round has been equal to that point, you should try to get the upper hand in the last 30 seconds. Then the jury members might award the round to you.

It's better to shout "Chico" than "Half a minute to go", as the opponent and his corner will understand this as well. Now you hear a lot of gyms shouting "Chico" towards the end of a round and they have no idea what it actually means. Chico was the name of Rik van de Vathorst's bull terrier. Back then I owned several bull terriers myself, but I liked the name "Chico". I said in class: "Chico is an easy name to pronounce and remember. We'll use the name of Rik's dog to signify the last 30 seconds of a round."

I would like to become more flexible and kick high, any advice? (answered by Julio Punch)

The best advice I can give you is to join a power yoga class several times a week. Power yoga is an athletic form of yoga and most commercial gyms offer classes. If you can't find power yoga, any form of hatha yoga will do. If classes under an instructor are not an option, Shiva Rea's and Mark Blanchard's DVDs are very good, but there are other excellent DVDs out there.

Although age and genetics play a role, anyone can increase his or her flexibility with consistent practice. You won't need expensive supplements or need to change your training schedule every few weeks like you would do with weight training. Unlike strength, speed and endurance training, it's impossible to overtrain in stretching. So if flexibility is your goal and you have the time, you could make it a daily ritual.

DISCLAIMER. The authors cannot be held responsible for any injuries that may result from the use or misuse of the fighting, training or nutrition advice contained in this book. Please consult your physician before changing your diet or exercise schedule.

A HISTORY IN PICTURES

The ship Oranjefontein. The ship was built in 1940 and demolished in 1967. Picture: www.vns-voe.nl

Thom Harinck, far right, in his army days in 1962.

Soccer team with Thom Harinck sitting second from left. This was a team of waiters and bouncers from clubs around Leidseplein in Amsterdam. It was named Lucky Star after the club of the same name where Thom Harinck worked as a bouncer in the late 1960s.

The Chakuriki style included the use of several Oriental weapons like the nunchaku seen in this picture from 1972.

Thom Harinck was already supplementing martial arts with weight training in the early 1970s, long before this became widely accepted.

The Chakuriki Emblem.

Chakuriki students sit in za-zen before a summertime demonstration in the early 1970s.

Holding up trophies after one of Charles Dumerniet's free fight events, early 1970s.

Dumerniet's free fight events in the early 1970s. Above: Chakuriki versus taekwondo. Below: Chakuriki versus pentjak-silat.

The different types of audiences at savate championships in France in 1975. The French crowd.

The different types of audiences at savate championships in France in 1975. The Dutch contingent.

Dutch team in training in Thailand, 1975.

Article in a newspaper in Thailand about the farang [foreigners] who had come to fight Thai opponents in 1975.

Thom Harinck coaching Kenneth Ramkisoen in Thailand, 1975.

Pandemonium in a Thai dressing room, 1975.

Thom Harinck and John de Ruiter at the first kickboxing event held in the Netherlands, 31 May 1976.

John Reeberg, member of the national karate team, came to the Chakuriki gym to prepare himself for a fight against Jan Kallenbach, Jon Bluming's top student, for the Dutch title in the late 1970s. Thom Harinck and John after he won his match.

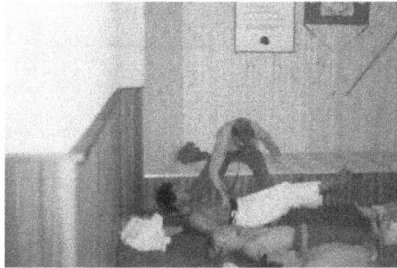

John Reeberg, member of the national karate team, came to the Chakuriki gym to prepare himself for a fight against Jan Kallenbach, Jon Bluming's top student, for the Dutch title in the late 1970s. John Reeberg training in the gym.

Performing the ibuki-nogare kata, a mysterious glow surrounds Thom Harinck's body (late 1970s).

SHIHAN
T HARINCk

Picture of Thom Harinck made by a student in the 1970s. He resembles Bodhidharma who is credited with bringing Zen Buddhism to China. Thom Harinck is credited with bringing muay thai to the West.

The late mahu guru of pentjak-silat, Frits Vermaesen, giving a demonstration with the tjabang (or sai), late 1970s. Picture: www.shwinongo.nl

The news of Iwan de Randamie's sad death in 1979 was featured in Dutch newspapers.

Richard Ploos, Dutch muay thai champion, 1979.

Thom Harinck demonstrating a low kick on Jan Plas of Mejiro Gym fame in 1981. Despite tension between the supporters of both gyms, the two senseis got along fine.

All of the students in this class are from minority groups (1981).

Second and third from left: Gilbert and Stuart Ballantine in their days of practicing wado-ryu karate, early 1980s.

Flyer for the Pankration event in Paradiso, 17 May 1981.

167

"Judo" Gene LeBell testing Thom Harinck's abs with one of his motor bikes, early 1980s.

Endurance training in the Amsterdam Woods, early 1980s.

Thom Harinck and pitbull in training, early 1980s.

Thom Harinck with Nonglek on his left and Fanta Attapong on his right. Both were famous muay thai champions in Thailand, early 1980s.

Mr Calendra (right) and Gerard Finot (left) in the early 1980s.

Thom Harinck has given many seminars in the USA. This was one of the first ones at Mike Anderson's gym in Florida in 1981.

Thom Harinck and Ron Kuyt demonstrating techniques typical of full contact or American kickboxing, 1981.

Thom Harinck and Ron Kuyt demonstrating French savate techniques, 1981.

Rik van de Vathorst and Arthur Klootwijk (far right) with the next generation of Thai ring warriors in the early 1980s.

The statue of Dieselnoi's famous match against Samart in 1982 received from Mr. Montri Mongkosawat (manager of the Rajadamnern Stadium) for Harinck's improvements to the sport. It reads: "With the best compliment from Montri Mongkolswat, deputy manager, Rajadamnern Stadium, Bangkok, Thailand".

The painting of Dieselnoi's famous match against Samart in 1982 received from Mr. Montri Mongkosawat (manager of the Rajadamnern Stadium) for Harinck's improvements to the sport.

172

Thom and Tommie Harinck, early 1980s.

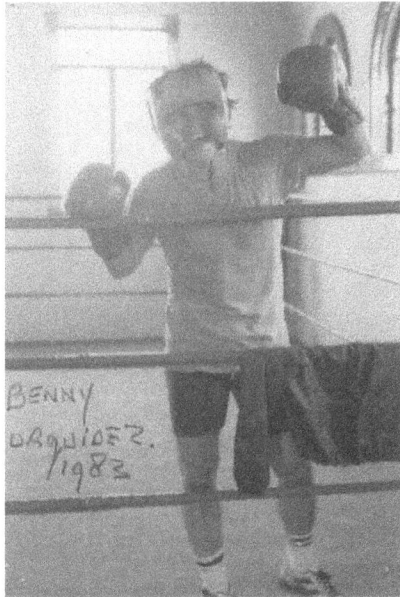

Benny "The Jet" Urquidez at the Chakuriki gym in 1983.

Flyer for kickboxing event with Benny Urquidez, 15 January 1984.
Lucia "Striker" Rijker won her first world title that night.

Ladies group in the mid 1980s. In the centre Saskia van Rijswijk
(with the blue top) and on her left Corrine Geeris.

Rik van de Vathorst and coach, 1985.

Benny "The Jet" Urquidez and Thom Harinck at the famed "Jet Center" (now defunct) in Los Angeles in 1985.

The Dutch team with Carter Wong, star of Big Trouble in Little China, in Hong Kong in the mid 1980s.

The Chakuriki team on a boat in the harbour of Hong Kong, mid 1980s.

Saskia van Rijswijk, world champion muay thai and movie star in 1985. Picture: Saskia van Rijswijk.

Tekin Donmez, Thom Harinck's best pupil of all time in 1986.

Willem Ruska, Thom Harinck and Chris Dolman in Amsterdam's Red Light District in 1988. The loft of Amsterdam's most famous sex club housed a martial arts gym for 16 years.

Stuart Ballantine after winning the European KICK title in the late 1980s.

Thom Harinck and Kenneth Plak, late 1980s.

Gilbert Ballentine after his KO win against Thomas Seiler, 24 April 1990. Far right: Seiler's coach Detlef Turnau.

Thom Harinck dining with Bob "O'Hara" Wall and his family in 1990.

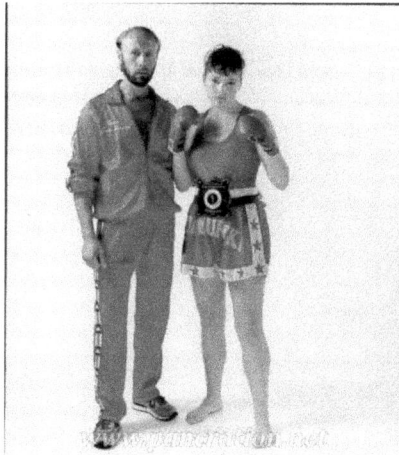

Thom Harinck and Corrine Geeris, 1990.

General meeting International Muay Thai Association in 1990.
Thom Harinck founded the NKBB (Dutch Kickboxing Association)
in 1976, the MTBN (Dutch Muay Thai Association) in 1983, the
WMTA (World Muay Thai Association) and the EMTA
(European Muay Thai Association).

A reverse punch (gyaku tsuki) typical for competition karate made
by Ino Alberga, teacher of shotokan karate in 1991.

Thom Harinck with Gerard "Sifu" Meijers , AKA Prince Dschero
Khan. who popularised shaolin kempo in the Netherlands and
Germany in the 1960s and 1970s. The picture was taken at a
martial arts event in 1991.

The coach and his champions. From left to right: Gilbert Ballantine, Peter Aerts and Branko Cikatiç in 1992.

Thom Harinck in Mexico in 1993, a country he enjoyed visiting a lot.

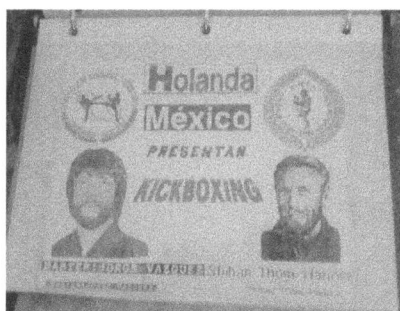

Promotion material for the matches in Mexico in 1993.

Thom Harinck and Perry Ubeda, early 1990s.

Thom Harinck with Peter Aerts and Rob Kaman, first Dutch WKA-champion, early 1990s.

Elation in the Chakuriki camp after Branko became the first K-1 champion, 30 April 1993. (I)

Elation in the Chakuriki camp after Branko became the first K-1 champion, 30 April 1993. (II)

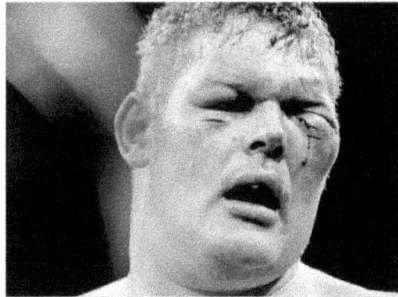

This is how Ruud Ewoldt looked like after his fight against Yoshishu Yamamoto, 19 February 1995. This picture led to an investigation by the Minister of Sports, Erica Terpstra. Picture: www.hansheus.nl.

Patrik "The Fighting Viking" Eriksson after his win in South-Africa, 26 May 1996. On the left K-1 fighter Mike Bernardo.

From left to right: Stephen Tapilatu, Pati Tapilatu, Perry Ubeda, coach Thom Harinck and Wijnand Tapilatu in 1996 when Perry won the Open Japan Taekwondo Championship.

Peter Aerts (middle), Andy Hug and a Japanese fan, late 1990s.

Nobu Hayashi before a match in Japan, late 1990s.

Artwork on the walls of Pancration gym, founded by Thom Harinck and Chris Dolman in 2002.

Flyer for the event where a young Badr Hari would face England's Gary Turner in 2004.

A young Badr Hari (second to the right) anked by Melvin Manhoef in 2004.

Menno Dijkstra after his fight against K-1 Max champ Albert Kraus on 18 December 2005. On Menno's left Kraus' coach Dennis Krauweel.

Judo is great for kids. All of Thom Harinck's children have trained in judo. Tobias (with the curly hair) is in the front row . Next to him Charlotte with the orange belt. Jane on the far right with blue belt (2006).

Ginty Vrede on his way to the ring in Las Vegas, where he would become world champion by defeating Shane Rosario in 2008. Picture: Harmen Bakker.

Nobu Hayashi and Thommie Harinck after Nobu's release from hospital in 2010.

Peter Aerts warming up for a fight in Japan in 2010. On the left: Nobu Hayashi.

Concentration before the fight with Peter Aerts in 2010

Nobu, Peter Aerts and Thom Harinck in Japan, 2010.

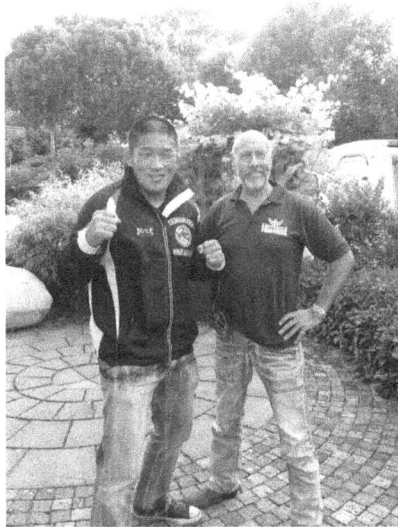

Thom Harinck with Satoshi Ishii, MMA fighter from Japan in 2010.

Thom Harinck with Jérôme Le Banner on their way to the ring, 2010.

Le Banner beats Tyrone Spong, K-1 World Grand Prix, Yokohama, Japan, 4 March 2010.

Reunion with Don "The Dragon" Wilson in 2010.

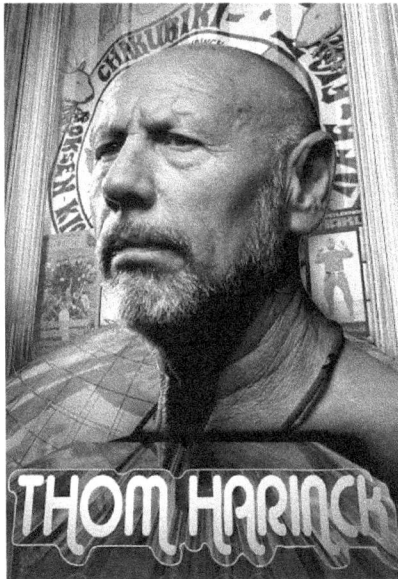

Picture of Thom Harinck made by a Dutch artist in 2010.

Chakuriki team spirit in a Japanese dressing room, 2011.

Thom Harinck and Chris Dolman, mates for life, 2012.

The family together on the day Thom Harinck's wife became professor, 1 May 2012.

All my champions together in 2012. From left to right: Atje Smit (assistant), Jérôme Le Banner, Hesdy Gerges, Marjan Olfers, Raoel Catinas, Amir Zeyada, Thommie Harinck, Satosh Ishii, and Bruno from Brazil.

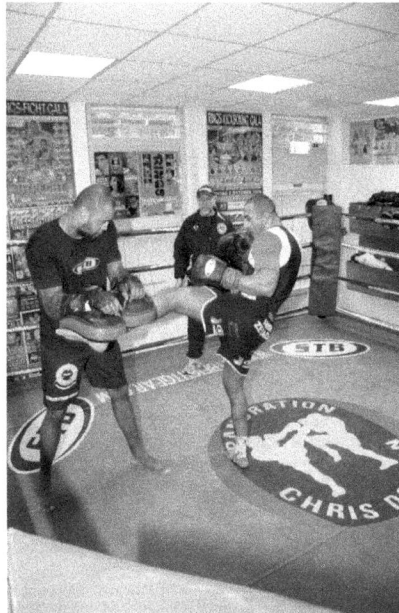

Amir Zeyada on the pads with Hesdy Gerges, 2012.

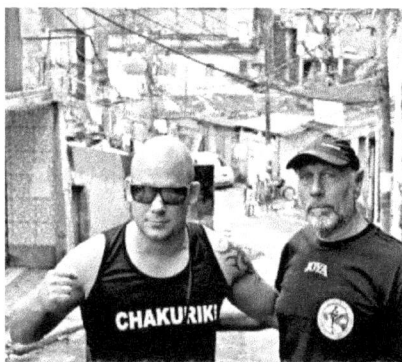

Thom Harinck and Menno Dijkstra in the slums of Brazil, 2012.

Thom Harinck and Ramon Dekkers shortly before his untimely death in 2012.

Thom Harinck at age 70 in a traditional gi in 2012.

Hesdy Gerges wins in Japan, 21 December 2012.

Thom Harinck with wife, kids, Menno Dijkstra and Patrik Eriksson, showing gifts he received when he retired from coaching in 2013.

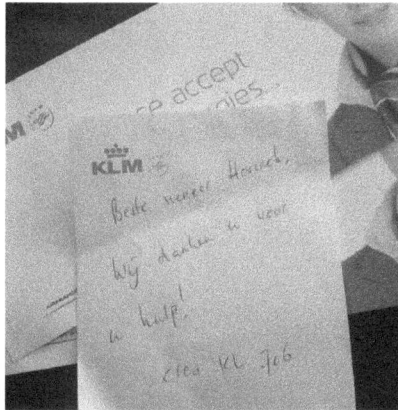

*The letter from KLM to Thom Harinck after the incident in 2014
with the drunk Englishman. In Dutch it says: "Dear Mr. Harinck.
We thank you for your help! Crew KL. 706".*

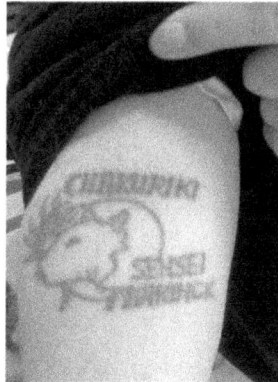

Many Chakuriki students sport Chakuriki tattoos.

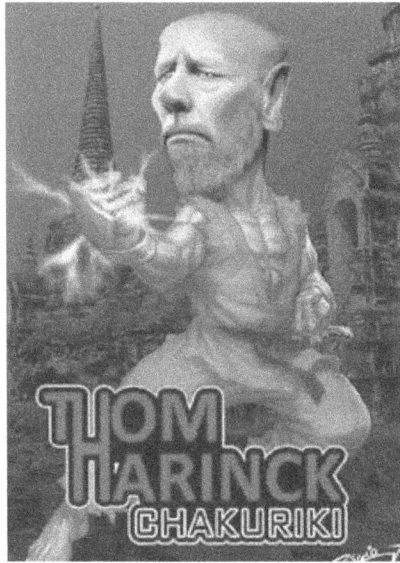

Picture of Thom Harinck, made by a Brazilian fan in 2014.

Inducted into the martial arts hall of fame in 2014.

One of the many awards Thom Harinck got for his involvement in the martial arts. This one from 2015 even awarded him academic titles.

APPENDIX A: CHAMPIONS AND OTHER IMPORTANT PEOPLE

CHARLES DUMERNIET

Charles Nicolaas Dumerniet was born in The Hague in 1929. From an early age he cross-trained in a variety of martial arts, including judo, jiu-jitsu, kyokushinkai karate and pentjak-silat pukulan. Dumerniet introduced the "Free-fight" concept in 1968 and the first competition was held in 1973, open to all styles of martial arts. Disenchanted with the traditional and non-innovative approach to martial arts of the BBN (*Budo Bond Nederland*/Dutch Budo Organization), he founded his own International Martial Arts Organization, or IOG (*Internationale Organisatie Gevechtskunsten*).

The first issue of the all-round martial arts magazine *Samurai* was published by Dumerniet in 1973. The free-fight events he organized remained popular until around 1979. At the beginning of the 1980s, however, his free-fight concept faded into obscurity. Charles Dumerniet stated in 1992: "When Jan Plas and Thom Harinck introduced kickboxing in the Netherlands, something was set in motion that couldn't be stopped. In some ways, it was a continuation of free-fight, you could call it the next step. If you look at Thom Harinck's club, for example, you will see that all his kickboxing champions got their competitive start in their red uniforms at the events that I organized."

Charles Dumerniet continued teaching martial arts in his home town of The Hague until his death in 2000.

SASKIA VAN RIJSWIJK

Saskia van Rijswijk was born in Amsterdam in 1961. In the local swimming pool, she encountered Chakuriki fighter Ron Kuyt. When she asked him about his abdominal muscles, he pointed her to the Chakuriki Dojo. As a thirteen-year-old, she entered the Chakuriki Dojo for the first time. Having gained ring experience in full-contact matches, she became world champion in muay thai on 20 September 1981 by defeating her Thai opponent Yupin Chotchai. She retired from competition shortly thereafter, but continued training kickboxing to stay in shape. She served as a jury member for muay thai competitions internationally and gave many demonstrations at martial arts events in the 1980s.

She became European Champion of disco dancing in 1986, and authored an aerobics video along the lines of Billy Blank's Tae-bo, before Blanks had even coined the term Tae-bo. She was centerfold in the Dutch edition of *Playboy Magazine* in 1987. She studied Psychology at a later age and is now a mental coach. To this day, she credits the discipline she learned in the Chakuriki Dojo as a major factor of her success in many different endeavors.

Saskia's acting career began in 1984 with a small role in the Dutch movie *De Ratelrat* (The Rattle Rat). She starred in several Hong Kong produced action movies that were successful in Hong Kong and Thailand. She trained with Appy Echteld (former European pentjak-silat champion and National karate coach) and his Kiai-do team to prepare for the fight scenes.

Filmography:

- De ratelrat (1987)
- Final Run (1989)
- Midnite Angels III (1989)
- China White (1989
- Fatal Mission (1991)

Saskia van Rijswijk can be reached at: www.saskiavanrijswijk.nl

GILBERT BALLANTINE

Gilbert "The Bull Terrier" Ballantine (pronounced like the whiskey brand of the same name), was born on 14 March 1961, in Paramaribo (capital of the former Dutch colony Suriname). He emigrated to the Netherlands as a young boy. His aggressive behavior at school led his mother to enroll him in judo classes. After attaining his blue belt, he switched to wado-ryu karate. Under the tutelage of Wim Massee, himself a student of 8th Dan Tatsuo Suzuki, he became a European wado-ryu karate champion and earned his black belt. He was also a member of the national karate team.

After earning his black belt in karate, Ballantine started training in kickboxing under Andre Brilleman, while continuing training karate. After Brilleman's untimely death, Ballantine trained for four years under Lucien Carbin, before enlisting at Amsterdam's Chakuriki Dojo in 1986. In his 12 years at the Chakuriki Dojo, Ballantine won nine world titles and four European titles in different forms of kickboxing. His fights against Milo el Geubli (1988) and Ramon Dekker (1989, 1992 and 1994) are legendary. His most notable win was probably the win on points against the Thai champion Sangtiennoi "The Deadly Kisser" Sitsurapong, in 1990. He fought his last kickboxing match in 2001 and continued with MMA matches up until his final departure from the ring in 2003. Ballantine currently teaches kickboxing classes at several gyms in the Amsterdam area. He can be reached at: www.gilbertballantine.com.

RIK VAN DE VATHORST

Rik van de Vathorst was one of the most popular Dutch fighters in the 1980s. His breakthrough came in 1985 with a win by KO against the hitherto considered unbeatable Fanta Attapong (world champion in muay thai). Fights against top Thai fighters like Nonglek and Krongsak followed later in his career. Rik fought for his own gym from 1988 onwards.

At a kickboxing event in 1991, Jan Wessels' opponent didn't show up. Rik, who was present as a spectator, offered to fight and save the main match of the evening, though he was unprepared. With his old coach Thom Harinck in his corner, he lost the match on points.

In 1984 Rik opened his gym in the west of Amsterdam, which he ran together with his parents, commonly known as "Auntie Hennie" and "Uncle Jan". The gym's most successful student is without a doubt, Ryan "Trubula" Simson. He trained at the gym for a total of 21 years, amassing five world titles and a number two ranking of the Lumpinee Stadium in Bangkok.

PERRY UBEDA

Perry Ubeda started kickboxing at the age of nine at a gym housed in the basement of a Chinese take-away restaurant called Chibo Gym. His trainer was Dick Veldhuis, himself a former student of Thom Harinck. Six months later, he also started training in kempo (also known as *kuntao* – a form of kung fu that came to the Netherlands via Indonesia), so he was able to train five times a week. He fought his first match at the age of ten.

The training at the gym was somewhat unorthodox. Perry said: "There was a older man nicknamed "Doughnut" (years later I learnt that his real name was Fred). He would call out the name of one of the tattoos on his torso and I would have to punch or kick the tattoo. He wanted me to be able to react fast and aim my punches and kicks well. I was the only kid in the group. All the others were 16 years or older. All these guys were pleased to be able to teach me things. That's the reason I became such a complete fighter during my ring career."

Perry fought for the Chakuriki Dojo from 1994 to 1998. He travelled by train from Nijmegen to Amsterdam three times a week, which cost him a small fortune. He had to fight at least one match a year to cover his travel expenses. He recalled: "Those were pleasant years and I learnt a lot. I had a lot of respect for Thom and I still have. I could always get along well with him." In total he won 13 championship titles in different martial arts.

Perry had his own gym for several years. He currently works with people with behavioral disorders, using martial arts as a means to vent aggression. Although Perry is one of Europe's most seasoned fighters, his father Joop has made more ring appearances. Joop Ubeda is one of the world's leading referees in kickboxing.

Having many shin injuries, during the last few years of his fighting career Perry switched to full contact or American kickboxing in which low-kicks are not allowed. By the year 2000 this form of kickboxing was as good as extinct in the Netherlands but still popular in several other European countries. Perry also became world champion in this form of kickboxing. After a few professional boxing matches, Perry fought his farewell match at Simon Rutz' It's Showtime event in Amsterdam Arena in 2009. Perry Ubeda can be reached at: www.perryubeda.nl.

PETER AERTS

Peter Aerts was born in 1970 and started training in taekwondo at the age of 13. Both his father and grandfather had fought boxing matches, but his mother wasn't keen on a fighting career for her son. He soon switched to kickboxing under Mickey BenAzzouz and fought his first match after one year of training. He later switched to The Champs gym owned by Eddy Smulders, former European champion boxing.

Peter's big success started after enlisting at the Chakuriki Dojo in

Amsterdam, winning the K-1 three times: in 1994, 1995 and 1998. During the first two of these, he was coached by Thom Harinck. From 1998 to 2009 Aerts held the record of the fastest K-1 Grand Prix win ever of 6.43 minutes. Aerts trained at several different gyms, including his home gym, from 2006 to 2009. Between 2009 and 2013 he was back at his old coach Thom Harinck. Peter Aerts fought the last matches of his career under the guidance of his first coach Mickey BenAzzouz. Peter Aerts retired in July 2015.

Since 2011 he made several appearances in show-wrestling events organized by Antonio Inoki.

Peter Aerts is a certified sports instructor and has his own gym, called the K-1 Aerts Dojo, in Enschede. He recently released his biography entitled "Peter Aerts: The Dutch Lumberjack". Peter has acted as himself in the movie *New Kids Turbo* and has appeared a total of 14 times in computer games. Peter Aerts can be reached at: www.k1-aerts-dojo.nl.

CHRIS DOLMAN

Chris Dolman was born on 17 February 1945. At the age of 16 he started to train in judo and karate under Jon Bluming. Bluming himself had recently come back from a long stay in Japan where he trained under kyokushinkai founder Mas Oyama and a host of judo luminaries at the Kodokan Dojo. Groundfighting was Dolman's forte and he became European Judo champion in 1966, and world champion Sambo in 1969. Sambo is a Russian version of Judo, and coincidentally the first style of Fedor Emilianenko, considered by many to be the greatest MMA-fighter of all time. Many national and international titles in judo and sambo would follow, equaling 50 titles in total.

During the last years of his career he became a regular competitor in *RINGS Japan*'s free-fight events. His last fight was against Akira Maeda in Amsterdam. The 50-year-old Dolman won by a leg lock.

Though his daughter Sharon has taken over the Pancration Gym, Dolman can still be found on the mat weekly.

BRANKO CIKATIĆ

Inspired by the Bruce Lee movies, the young Branko started training in Taekwondo as a 12-year-old boy. He achieved a black belt in this art. After boxing for several years and winning 16 of his 17 fights, he found his true calling in kickboxing. In the former Eastern Bloc-countries, amateur full-contact karate was very popular in the 1970s and 1980s. Forms of kickboxing with low-kicks were, at the time, frowned upon by the governments of the Eastern European countries.

As an amateur Cikatiç fought a total of 170 matches for the WAKO organization. 138 matches were won by knockout. In Miami Beach (USA) in 1981, he became world champion with the WAKO. He started fighting as a professional for the Chakuriki Gym in 1983, and became the first K-1 champion in 1993. Up until today he is the oldest K-1 champion. Cikatiç starred alongside Anne Nicole Smith in the movie *Skyscrapers*. Branko Cikatiç can be reached at: www.bcikatic.htnet.hr.

PATRIK ERIKSSON

Patrik Eriksson started with western boxing at the age of 13. Two years later he switched to Thai boxing. He fought his first match at the age of 17 and became champion of Sweden three years later. Patrik on his coach: "Thom Harinck can bring out the best in a fighter. He made me into the fighter that I am today. The training sessions are spartan. You can always train with top fighters in the gym and this is a great help. You stay on the edge of your game by constantly training with top fighters."

Titles:

1993 WMTA Swedish Champion

1996 Dutch Muay -Thai Champion

1996 WKA World Champion

1996 WMTA Europe Muay -Thai Champion

WKA World Kickboxing welter weight Champion

WMTA World Muay - Thai welter weight Champion

EMTA Europe Muay -Thai Champion

MENNO DIJKSTRA

Menno Dijkstra started out with judo as a young boy. He started training in kickboxing at the age of 16. After just one year of training he could advance to the competition group. He got his nickname from Thommie Harinck through his hard and fast combination on the pads. He became threefold Dutch champion (up to 70 kg), and in 2008 he became world champion against Brian lo an Njoe. He fought Albert Kraus (former K-1 Max champion) and lost on points. After winning the European Champion in 2010, Menno concentrated on a career as a personal trainer. He teaches weekly classes of bag training and kickboxing at Health City Premium in Amstelveen. Menno Dijkstra can be reached at: www.fitbyfight.com.

A complete list of champions trained by Thom Harinck

- Ron Kuyt - European champion muay thai
- Jhon de Ruiter - Dutch champion muay thai
- Robbie Schumann - European champion muay thai
- Gerard Bakker European champion WAKO kickboxing
- Iwan de Randamie - Dutch champion muay thai
- Roel de Graaf - European champion WAKO kickboxing
- Richard Ploos - Dutch champion muay thai
- Hans Monke - Dutch champion muay thai
- Feisal Karakus - Dutch champion muay thai / kickboxing

- Dennis Zeegers - Dutch champion muay thai
- Imro van Hetten - European champion muay thai / kickboxing
- Henk Rompa - European champion muay thai
- Gilbert Ballantine - World champion muay thai / kickboxing / full contact FFKA
- Stuart Ballantine - Dutch champion kickboxing
- Nick Bloemberg - European champion muay thai / kickboxing
- Kenneth Ramkisoen - European champion muay thai
- Muzaffer Yamali - Dutch champion muay thai
- Tekin Donmez - European champion muay thai / kickboxing
- André Tete - Dutch champion muay thai
- Perry Ubeda - European champion muay thai / kickboxing / full contact / world champion taekwondo / Dutch champion savate
- Peter Aerts - World champion muay thai / kickboxing / European champion full contact / 3 x K-1 champion
- Branko Cikatiç - World champion muay thai / kickboxing / full contact / 1 x K-1 champion
- Lloyds van Dams - European champion muay thai / kickboxing
- Clyde van Dams - Dutch champion muay thai
- Menno Dijkstra - European champion muay thai
- Amir Zeyada - European champion muay thai / kickboxing
- Hesdy Gerges - world champion muay thai and K-1 finalist
- Jan Lomulder - Dutch champion muay thai
- Pedro Rizzo
- Jérôme Le Banner
- Frank Muñoz
- Raul Catinas
- Saulo Cavalari
- Nobu Hayashi

- Anderson "Braddock" Silva - Brazilian champion kickboxing
- Patrik Eriksson - World champion kickboxing and muay thai
- Jan Lomulder - World champion muay thai, kickboxing and full contact.

APPENDIX B: A BRIEF OVERVIEW OF MARTIAL ARTS

JIU-JITSU

This is a Japanese self-defence art that uses throws, ground-fighting as well as kicks and punches. It was employed and developed by the samurai warriors in Medieval Japan for situations in which they couldn't use their weapons. A modern interpretation is Brazilian Jiu-jitsu which became popular after the Gracie family won multiple titles in the UFC (United Fighting Championships, see Mixed Martial Arts).

JUDO

Japanese educator Jigoro Kano (1860-1938) streamlined dozens of jiu-jitsu styles (or *koryo*) and came up with judo in 1882 - a martial art that uses mostly throws, locks and chokes. Judo became an Olympic sport in 1960. In 1964, the Dutch construction worker Anton Geesink (1934-2010) won Olympic gold, beating the Japanese at their own game. There was joy in millions of Dutch households when Geesink threw his opponent Akio Kaminaga to the mat in the finals and concluded the match with a stranglehold.

Just as the Bruce Lee movies triggered the "Kung Fu craze" in the early 1970s in the US, Geesink's Olympic gold medal in judo brought thousands, if not millions of people to judo clubs in the Netherlands. Judo was quickly stripped of its Eastern mystique, becoming a household word, and today remains one of the most popular sports for Dutch youngsters.

KARATE

Karate originated in Okinawa through the synthesis of several styles of Chinese martial arts from the mainland and martial art styles native to the island. Karate focuses, but is not limited to, punches and kicks. Popular styles are: shotokan, wado-ryu and kyokushinkai. The kyokushinkai style that was founded by Mas Oyama (1923-1994) has a reputation for Spartan training and full-contact competition. Kyokushinkai karate was introduced to the Netherlands by Jon Bluming. K-1 winner Andy Hug was a kyokushinkai champion before he turned to kickboxing, and Sem Schilt (4 times K-1 winner), trained in ashihara karate (which is an offshoot of kyokushinkai karate).

TAEKWONDO

A Korean martial art specifically known for its kicking techniques. Historically, the art is a Korean interpretation of shotokan karate, though the Koreans claim it derived from an ancient Korean art called "tai-kyon". Taekwondo in its full-contact form has been an Olympic sport since 2000.

KUNG FU

Kung Fu actually means "hard work" in Chinese, but is now used worldwide as an umbrella term for the various styles of Chinese martial arts. The number of styles worldwide is estimated to be around 400. Many styles of kung fu imitate the movements of animals like the tiger, crane, ape and the mythological dragon. The styles include external or hard styles that employ muscular strength such as hung gar and choy lee fut. The so-called internal or soft styles include hsing-i, pa-kua and tai chi and employ the inner strength known as *ch'i*. Many of the hard styles have Buddhist origins, while the soft styles have Taoist origins. The term wushu meaning "fighting arts" is used for a competition form in which forms (*kata* in Japanese) are performed and judged. The form was developed in Communist China and is considered to be more of a "martial ballet" than a true fighting art.

PENTJAK SILAT

Pentjak-silat (also spelled as pencak silat, literally "to fight like lightning") is an umbrella term for the fighting arts native to the Indonesian Archipelago. The exact number of styles is not known, but estimates vary from 150 to several hundreds. Styles differ from region to region, but many employ techniques that imitate the movements of animals, employ low stances, low foot sweeps and rapid hand movements to divert the opponent's attention.

In the years after Indonesia's independence in 1950, many Dutch people who resided in Indonesia, people of mixed Dutch and Indonesian blood (called *Indo's* in Dutch), and full-blooded Indonesians who had fought on the side of the colonial regime, emigrated to the Netherlands. The Netherlands has the largest Indonesian community outside of Indonesia itself. Among the immigrants from Indonesia were several "paks", the Indonesian term for martial arts masters. They started teaching in basements and attics in the 1950s and, keeping for the most part a low profile, in school gymnasiums in the 1960s and beyond.

While the graceful and lightning fast movements are a far cry from muay thai's brute power, the art of pentjak-silat has had an influence on the development of kickboxing in the Netherlands. World champion kickboxing Lucien Carbin trained under Frits Vermaesen (1929-1994) of the setia hati style, and coach Cor Hemmers of Golden Glory fame trained pukulan under Willem Flohr (1923-1998). Both kickboxing coaches cite their pentjak-silat gurus as an influence on their way of teaching.

KEMPO / KENPO

Kempo or kenpo (the Japanese characters are the same) is an umbrella term for martial arts of Chinese origin with a Japanese mark. There is shorinji kempo from Japan that is religiously inspired by Kongo Zen Buddhism and American kenpo karate developed by Ed Parker, who was taught by William Chow in Hawaii. The art which is known as kempo or shaolin kempo in the Netherlands and neighbouring countries, is a Japanese version of kuntao (kung fu that came to the Netherlands by Indonesia,) mixed with judo, jiu-jitsu and kyokushin karate. It was popularised in the 1960s and 1970s in the Netherlands and Germany by Gerard "Sifu" Meijers, also known as Prince Dschero Khan. This style bears the same name, but is unrelated to the shaolin kempo of Fred Villari, or the shaolin kenpo of Ralph Castro, both from the US.

KICKBOXING

A competitive form of martial arts in which all techniques are full-contact, i.e. can connect with maximum speed and power. Boxing gloves are mandatory and fights are held in a boxing ring. One can win by points or by knockout.

There are several rule sets:

Full-contact karate or American kickboxing: This form of kickboxing came about when practitioners of semi-contact karate competition started experimenting with training using boxing gloves in the early 1970s. Participants wear safe-T-kicks in addition to gloves. All kicks are above the belt and often a minimum number of kicks per round is required. No knees or elbows are allowed. For many years the PKA (Professional Karate Association) had a leading role in organising events for this form of kickboxing. Later, the WAKO (World All-Styles Karate Organisations) took over the leading role. Today this form of kickboxing is almost extinct in the Netherlands, but still popular in European countries like

Ireland and Italy. In North-America its popularity has been overshadowed by MMA.

WKA-rules: The World Karate Association was active from the late 1970s to the early1990s. Rules allowed kicking to the legs, but prohibited knees and elbows. The wearing of safe-T-kicks was mandatory.

Muay thai: Original muay thai rules are those used in Thailand, the art's country of origin. Rules allow use of the "eight limbs" to strike: feet, hands, knees and elbows. Clinching (body to body combat) is also allowed. Throws are prohibited, as is ground fighting.

K-1: These are basically muay thai rules without elbows. Extensive clinching is not allowed.

MMA (Mixed Martial arts)

A hybrid martial art that emerged out of full-contact competitions, with few rules held on several locations worldwide, pitting fighters of different martial arts against each other to see which style would emerge victorious. One thing that became clear was the effectiveness of grappling arts, illustrated by the multiple wins of the Gracie family that employed *Brazilian Jiu-jitsu*. What we now know of MMA is a sport in itself in which the participants train and use striking and kicking arts, as well as various ground-fighting arts. Competitions are often held in a cage called an Octagon. The UFC (Ultimate Fighting Championships) are currently the biggest MMA organisation worldwide and organise events on a monthly basis.

SAVATE

Savate is said to have originated when French sailors engaging in fisticuffs as a past time, had to use their hands to hold onto boat railings, to be able to kick. Hence, the many high kicks in savate. Later, western boxing was added to the curriculum and Europe's first and only kickboxing art was born. The first official savate gym was opened in France in 1825. Now the art is practised in 40 different countries worldwide. Competitors wear boxing gloves, shoes and a special track suit.

SAMBO

A Russian interpretation of judo, with slightly different rules and clothing.

APPENDIX C: LIST OF STADIUMS

Jaap Edenhal / Jaap Eden Hall – Hall in the eastern part of Amsterdam with ice-rink. Hundreds of kickboxing events were held there, including the first in 1976 and up to 2005.

Sporthallen Zuid / Sport Halls South – Halls in the southern part of Amsterdam. It was a home base for the organisation *RINGS Holland* for many years.

Vechtsebanen – Sports hall in Utrecht, The Netherlands.

Ahoy – Large, multi-purpose arena in Rotterdam (The Netherlands). It was the home of *2Hot2Handle* martial arts events for several years.

Amsterdam Arena – Largest, and multi-purpose, stadium in the Netherlands, located in the south east of Amsterdam. Home to Ajax Football Club. It was the exclusive home to Simon Rutz Promotions' *It's Showtime* events from 2003 until 2010. (Nowadays this arena is called: Johan Cruijff Arena).

Rajadamnern Stadium – One of two large sports arenas in Bangkok (Thailand) known for muay thai matches. The other stadium being the Lumpinee Stadium. This stadium has its own ranking for the sport of *muay thai*. Capacity: 8,000 people.

Lumpinee Stadium – One of two large sports arenas in Bangkok (Thailand) known for *muay thai* matches. The other stadium being the Rajadamnern stadium. The Lumpinee stadium is owned by the Thai Army and has its own ranking. Capacity: 9,500 people.

Tokyodome – Large arena in Tokyo (Japan) that has places for 55,000 spectators. It's most often used for baseball matches, but music concerts and martial arts events are also held there. Up until 2006 it was the home for the K-1 Grand Prix. After 2006 this was held in the Yokohama Arena.

Van Hogendorphal – Hall in south Amsterdam, home to Erwin van der Meulen's *Victory or Hell* events.

Deutschlandhalle – Sports hall in Berlin (Germany), home to the WAKO championships of 1974 and 1975. The building was demolished in 2011. An ice hockey hall now stands in its place.

Yoyogi Stadium – Sports hall in Tokyo (Japan) used mainly for basketball and ice hockey competitions. It can host 10,500 people.

APPENDIX D: LIST OF JAPANESE TERMS

Oesh: used as a general affirmative in the Japanese martial arts.

Sensei: teacher, sometimes shortened to "sen" by Chakuriki students

Kancho: founder of a martial arts style.

Dojo: literally "place where the 'Way' is practised". Most often used to refer to martial arts gyms, but can also refer to locations where *za-zen* is practised.

Gi: uniform used for practising martial arts.

Za-zen: literally: sitting meditation. This is done before and after class in most Japanese martial arts.

Kata: a pre-arranged set of techniques of a fight against one opponent or more opponents that is performed solo.

Mondo: used in Zen Buddhism for a dialogue of questions and answers between student and master.

Makiwara: a padded striking post used in many karate styles. Said to be the "soul of karate" by Masatoshi Nakayama, master of shotokan karate.

COLOPHON

Title: Thom Harinck - Godfather of Muay Thai Kickboxing in the West

Authors: Thom Harinck & Julio Punch

ISBN 13: 9789492371485 (eBook)

ISBN 13: 9789492371072 (paperback)

Copyright text © Thom Harinck & Julio Punch, 2016

Introduction: Roger Price and Maurice Punch

Proofreading: Corry and Maurice Punch, and Roger Price

Published by: Amsterdam Publishers The Netherlands in 2016

Photographs: All pictures are from Thom Harinck's private collection unless stated otherwise. We would like to thank Hans Heus, Harmen Bakker, Motoyuki Amai, Saskia van Rijswijk, John van der Spek and Paul Tolenaar for kindly allowing us to use their photographs.

Photographer front cover: Paul Tolenaar

For press enquiries and enquiries about foreign rights, please get in touch with Liesbeth Heenk at info@amsterdampublishers.com

About the authors:

Thom Harinck (The Netherlands, 1943) lives in Amsterdam and is married to Marjan Olfers. Thom and Marjan have three children: Jane, Charlotte and Tobias. Thom is the author of four books on martial arts. He can be reached at: www.thomharinck.com

Julio Punch (United Kingdom, 1971) is a translator and computer instructor from the Amsterdam area. He has practised several martial arts as well as yoga: he has a blue belt in kyokushinkai karate. He studied Philosophy and Cultural Anthropology at the Free University of Amsterdam. The current publication is his first book, but he has written a number of articles on Native Americans. He can be reached at: www.julio-online.net

Lightning Source UK Ltd.
Milton Keynes UK
UKHW022021140819

347975UK00013B/365/P

9 789492 371072